"There are few people I respect more than Anji Barker. For decades, she has been putting flesh on the Good News of Jesus. This intimate book reads like a diary, with scrapnotes and stories of God at work in the world, through ordinary people who choose to do life a little differently. If you want to see what a life devoted to Jesus and the mission of God looks like, read this book, and follow Anji Barker. For two decades I've followed her and Ash from Australia to Bangkok to Birmingham. We've tracked through open sewage and chased runaway llamas. Every moment is an adventure, and every page of this book is a gem."

– Shane Claiborne, author, activist, and co-founder
of Red Letter Christians

First published in Great Britain in 2021

Published by Seedbeds Communications
Seedbeds.org

Cataloguing-in-Publication information available at
National Library of Australia

Barker, Anji
Missionary Not Just A Position

ISBN 978-0-6484725-2-0 (paperback)

Layout & pre-press by Splitting Image Colour Studio Pty Ltd,
Victoria, Australia

Printed by IngramSpark

MISSIONARY

NOT

JUST

A

POSITION

Anji Barker

This book is dedicated to all the many amazing team mates and volunteers that have been part of making this life, and these stories possible. You Rock!! There are so many of you in Australia, Thailand and the UK that continue to work tirelessly for a better world.

Let us not become weary of doing good for at the proper time we will reap a harvest if we do not give up.

The Bible (Galatians 6:9)

Special Thanks

To my family Ash, Aiden, Amy and Rob who are my life. I love you more than any words can express.

To Sally Mann and Jessica Craig who gently forced me to sit still long enough to get this written, and who encourage and inspire me daily with the way they live whole heartedly for their community.

And last but not least to the amazing Debbie Oakes who has brilliantly edited and shaped the final outcome of this book – despite going through her own dislocation from Asia and the pain that comes with that.

Foreword

Bangkok, 14 April 2013

When the month of April reaches out its sticky fingers no amount of complaining stops its unwelcome advances. Not even a whisper of sweet nothings breaks the stagnant monotony of Bangkok's relentless tropical heat. Along with most city-dwellers I shelter at home – or in one of the many palatial shopping malls – surrounded by the cool comfort of available air-con.

Today I am awake early (to avoid the midday sun) to follow mosaic artist, Cheryl Stansfield into Bangkok's Klong Toey slum. Cheryl has been spending most of her spare time in the heart of it all, involved with various projects organised by fellow Aussies – missionaries – she calls the 'incredible Barkers'. Her tales have made me laugh, made me cry and left me deeply intrigued and excited to be interviewing Anji Barker for a magazine article I am working on.

Even the first light of morning seems reluctant as it squeezes through the urban smog to reach us. On Sukhumvit Road, luxury condos, shining temple stupas, golden spirit houses and ever present traffic slowly wake as we hail a tuk tuk. In only 2kms – yet a world away – the voluminous shiny malls and designer hair-dos of central Sukhumvit give way to an altogether dustier, ragged and rubbish strewn reality. Over the lawnmower roar of Bangkok's ubiquitous motorised three-wheeler, I think about 'missionaries' I imagine slow-boiling bespectacled Brits in another time – bashing bibles on the heads of indigenous tribes. OK – I'm a Kiwi, but 'Australian missionaries' just seems like a contradiction in terms! Just who are these 'incredible Barkers' that have voluntarily made their home in a most unlikely place – a baking slum?

Cheryl has told me about the schools, the grassroots business development, healthcare and youth programs. The Barkers are, by her no-nonsense account, helping their neighbours raise their lot in life.

As we weave carefully to their little slum home, open sewers join together with canals (klongs) alongside the narrow alleyways, which generously sharing their noxious odours. Fanged wildlife scuttle and slither past clucking chickens, crying babies and spotless little girls with perfect pigtails.

Most of the approx. 100,000 slum-dwellers are descendants of poor migrants who came from Thailand's impoverished North East to build Bangkok's Port in the 1950's. They then stayed to work as manual labourers, illegally occupying land owned by the Thai Port Authority. It was originally a win/win situation as employers had a large pool of cheap labour and the workers had accommodation near their jobs.

Then I see her in the distance. Blonde hair swinging as she chats 90 to the dozen with her young assistant. Pretty, younger (and much less Victorian) than I imagined, Anji Barker is as true-blue Aussie as a heartfelt chorus of *Waltzing Matilda*. She flips between (what sounds to me like) pitch-perfect Thai and Aussie vernacular. She jokes: "The chicks I used to visit in jail called me the swearing nun," Her husband, Ash Barker is running around coaching the soccer team he helps run on the ragged concrete with happy, excited, carefree boys. Serious and proud in their little uniforms.

As we watch them play Anji begins to tell me that, together with Ash, they founded a charity to live amongst and help communities on (or under) the poverty line. "We have been grossed out at times and we don't use the 'M' (missionary) word because that can mean, 'Come! We'll force you to convert – and then we'll help you ... Are we Christians? Yes. But converting people is not our primary aim. That's between an individual and God. We help anyone in our path. It is not for me to force anyone to do anything; just be the best example of a Christian I can! We took a vow of poverty so that we could try to understand the pressures of those we live amongst – but we know we can never truly understand. Also – if we have to raise only limited funds for ourselves – it frees up more money for all other projects."

And projects, I discover, there are many. Anji explains, "For us it is not just about programs, and structures, but relationships with the people themselves. All of the projects, started out as raw need." She tells me about what – at that moment in time – was the most urgent need: a soccer program. It seems emblematic of their approach. "If we don't get funding it will be shut down", she says passionately. "Sport programmes provide a healthy, positive outlet for energy – and release of traumatic stress. Of course, the kids love it and happiness is wonderful in its own right. But also because they are learning how to connect with each other, how to resolve issues, and exercise self discipline. They aren't on the streets. Let's face it there is not a lot to do here. If the kids aren't here we really worry about them. Some disappear for a few months – lured into sniffing glue. They get arrested and when they get out they come back. Very much better for them than the alternatives! Children growing up in poverty are easily led into crime and drugs. Our greatest hope for these kids is for life outside the slum. They might choose to always live here – but they also might choose to experience life – have a real job outside. Obviously, as Christians, we hope people will be truly transformed … that they can find meaning and self-esteem and security beyond this crazy slum world. And that the knock-on effect will transform more lives."

Anji goes on to tell me that they moved from a poor part of Melbourne and everywhere the social issues of poverty are the same. "The main disparity is that the consequences of poverty in slums like Klong Toey, are massive. There is no safety net. At home – there is always somewhere to go for free food. Here, if you don't have money, there is no food for your kids. But poverty is not just a lack of money. It can be loneliness, mental health issues, low self-esteem. You could throw a million dollars at the poverty in Klong Toey and the people would be poor tomorrow. With money alone you are not solving the lack of education, nutrition, skills, good-decision making, and ability to hold healthy relationships. Cash alone will not fix this. It takes people to be there on the journey with them, to create possibility from within to create change."

And there it was. The moment I understood what a missionary was. Or what it is to Anji. I understood who the 'incredible Barkers' were. These are the people who are truly prepared to 'Be the change'.

For most of us change creeps in through the secret little crevices of our lives and sets about rearranging the furniture. It shades the internal landscape so subtly, there is barely a hint anything is happening and before you know it – tragedy and love; death and birth; betrayal and truth have unfolded before our eyes. People respond to change in many unconscious, often primal, ways. Some run for cover, ducking and diving behind the security of routine, habit and structured lives. Others embrace it as their escape route from responsibility or expectation.

But, more than anyone I have ever met, Anji taught me something that humid day. And, even though she speaks a 100 words a minute, it was not just what she said but rather, who she quintessentially is. And it is this: transformation is a little different: transformation is what occurs if you have enough faith to jump on the back of change and ride it like a bucking bronco. Transformation happens even if you don't believe in yourself but have the courage to act anyway. Transformation happens when you have faith in God, or the Universe (or whatever) to drop the reins of fear and embrace love.

The 'incredible Barkers' live and breathe 'love thy neighbour' the same way that I breathe air. Anji is one of those people that exemplify grace in the world. Someone you meet and feel like your karma might have just improved slightly for knowing her. She has shown me that change is nothing to fear and transformation can be a force of something mighty good in the world.

Debbie Oakes, London, 14 April 2021

Prequel

A steady stream of water is filling up the pool and suddenly I need to pee. My decaf coffee tastes strange, and isn't helping the situation. Wrinkling my nose, I squirm in and effort to both drink it and hold on. The cup is hot in the warm sun and I reflect – life is often just like that – we are inevitably trying to suck something up and just hold on. I think back on all the adventures of my life, quietly thanking God I'm still here. Still in one piece and able to tell the tales. How did an Aussie girl from sunny Melbourne end up living in another world, deep in the heart of Birmingham?

I wonder what – if anything – have I learnt along the way?

It is late September. The summer heat has departed with the majority of tourists; so there really are no distractions and no excuses. Try as they might to tempt me from my purpose – the warm blue waters and soaring cliffs of this Greek Island are no competition for the fierce women who are with me. My amazing, much-loved mother-in-law, Mary has brought me on the holiday of a lifetime. I tease her that she's the Birthday Wish Fairy taking the sting out of the big 5-0. And with us are, Jess Craig and Sally Mann, two friends from London's East End. They have formed a loving gang around me. Their mission is to make sure I don't wriggle out of the task at hand. After a couple of false starts, a few failed attempts and a number of empty promises that: 'I'll write my book as soon as life calms down a bit,' we are all here to finally make it happen. It's the perfect excuse and the perfect birthday gift. One thing is for certain – without distance from the everyday chaos of life in Birmingham – it would not get written. Here, at least, I stand a fighting chance of sitting still long enough to get something down. This awful decaf better be worth it! I feel so lucky, so blessed to have these two incredible friends who seem even more committed to telling my story than I am. I also ask myself, not for the first time, how did I get to have the world's best, mother-in-law? Still zany enough at 74 to 'get her motor running' on the back of a motorbike and zoom around Santorini with me?

We have devised a cunning system. Every morning Jess and Sally interview me with questions about my life. They then spend hours each day transcribing my words. A journalist once told me I speak more than 100 words a minute and my poor friends are now dealing with my ninety-to-the-dozen mind. Having this structure allows a framework to contain my hyperactive brain. It gives me an organised base to actually write from. I am trying not to feel too bad laying in the Grecian sunshine, taking heart in the fact that there's no pleasure in the decaf as their keyboards tap, tap, tap in the shade. All these stories are so emotional, so precious I realise that in the telling, their resonance affects me still. I'm not good with emotion. Everyone who knows me, knows that. So, in an attempt to look a little less like a slacker, I distract myself by I scribbling serious life notes in a fluffy neon-pink notebook with fabulous matching pen given to me by my teammate, Louise. I can relate to the pompom at the end of the pen as it bobs up and down. A ridiculous and fitting way to share my adventures. The pool is full now and I remember I have to run and pee!

When people ask me what I do for a living, I usually say social worker, or community worker, or sometimes 'the Vicar's wife'. Occasionally I'll say I'm a missionary because it's funny. I love to watch people raise their eyebrows and look me up and down. I guess I'm not what people expect when you say the 'm' word. Yet recently, more than ever, I think it actually describes best what I do. Tattoos and a bit of rough language aside, I do feel on a mission. Driven to change my little part of the world. I feel called, compelled even, to be a sign of hope and light in dark places. You will find me where injustice and poverty cause suffering and pain. Does that sound arrogant? I hope not, because I don't believe it is within my power to do this alone. It is my belief that it is only God that can bring about change. I just get to go along for the ride. It is my intention to be instrumental – a part of God's grace – in bringing about change in my small corner of this hurting world. I truly believe that is why I was born. I have tried a few times to escape and found that you can run but cannot hide from your life's purpose.

Acknowledgements

I want to acknowledge that, just as it "takes a village to raise a child", it took a number of actual villages to allow me to be the protagonist of these stories. It would be impossible to acknowledge all the players without hundreds more pages. But to get one thing straight – I have only been able to live these adventures because of so many amazing people. Nothing I have been a part of has been solely my own doing. Everything was inspired by or learnt from working in collaboration with many unsung heroes ... who should all write books themselves!

There is one group of people however, that I want to single out. I want to thank them the most. These are the many people who have financially supported Ash and I over the past 30 years. These are the behind-the-scenes essential enablers of our mission. The people who go to work every day, sometimes to jobs they hate, are true heroes. They have faithfully given their hard-earned money (and other practical support) no strings attached to Ash and I and our mission over the years. Let me tell you – living on the donations of others is incredibly humbling. It is scary, and at times, a humiliating way of life. It has kept me on my toes and driven me to try and work in a way worthy of everyone's sacrifice. To all those people: I hope you feel that this work and these stories are your legacy. I also want to thank every single person who has prayed for and encouraged us over the years.

This book is an honest account of it all. How sometimes I have messed up and struggled. At times I have been well-meaning but made misguided attempts to live out my calling. I feel concerned that when stories are told out of context there is a risk of them morphing into the realm of urban legend; a little truth, a little myth, a few romanticised add-ons. But it is my goal to stay as true as possible to the events as I remember them ... whilst recognising that the memory fades and details can sometimes get confused. I am over 50 after all!

Introduction

Bangkok, 26 January 2005

Many months of negotiations have culminated in this moment. I'm so nervous I find myself shivering in the heat of Bangkok's watery midday sun. My friend Thida, clings tightly to her 6-month old baby as the police load her into the back of the barred police truck. Catching a glimpse of two Indian men already inside, hands and feet shackled together, I realise the shock of seeing humans chained like that will stay with me forever. I'm holding my breath as the doors slam shut behind her. Smile frozen on my face, I climb into the front of the truck and unconsciously bounce my 15 month old baby, Aiden on my lap. He begins making funny faces at the police officers which seems to diffuse the seriousness of the situation and they actually smile and play along with him. We are on our way to Suvarnabumi International Airport – or so I hope! Finally, I managed to convince the Immigration Police to arrest Thida so she could be deported rather than languish, stateless, in Bangkok eternally. I reflect that the real trick has been to get her expelled with her child, an Australian citizen, to Australia. Not – God forbid – to the Burmese border. Aiden and I are escorting her because, not speaking English, she needs help. Having a foreign onlooker also ensures the police do not mistreat her. So much planning has gone into this but now the moment is finally here, I am deeply worried. Will the Thai Police honour their promise to take us to Suvarnabumi? Or were we headed somewhere more 'distasteful' with our little children?

Thida is the wife of Paul, a Burmese-Australian friend. Paul managed to escape to Australia following the 1988-1990 pro-democracy uprising in Burma. Just like the tragic stories unfolding today; there were student strikes and demonstrations. Followed by the torture and death of democracy activists standing against SLORC – the Military Junta. Aung San Suu Kyi made her first public speech in 1988 and the National League for Democracy (NLD) opposition party was formed. In the 1990 elections the NLD won by a landslide but SLORC refused to honour the results of the elections. Instead NLD politicians and student activists were rounded up, imprisoned, tortured or simply disappeared. Many fled over the border into Thailand where they sought (and continue to seek) United Nations High Commissioner for Refugees (UNHCR) protection. From Thailand they were accepted as refugees to countries such as Denmark, America and Australia. Many exiled politicians and activists became our neighbours in the Melbourne suburb of Springvale where Ash and I lived.

Over time a number of these refugees came to live with us in our home (and refuge) in Melbourne. We found the Burmese people we met to be humble and gentle natured ... which makes the ongoing cruelty and torture by the military incongruous and impossible to comprehend.

One of young men had been staying with us for six months when we realised what a significant player he had been in the student uprising. He was no less than one of Burma's eight most wanted! Still a close friend of ours today, he continues to fight for the freedom of his long suffering people. Another guy who stayed with us was Aung San Suu Kyi's body guard. Whatever your opinion of her, and her movement, the Military Junta has not changed. As I write this they have begun targeting children at the protests; shooting them in the head.

I met Paul, and his heavily pregnant wife Thida, during the first two years we lived in Bangkok. Our Burmese friends in Australia put us in touch with members of the NLD in Thailand and I began teaching English to the exiled activists and helped with a multitude of immigration and sponsorship forms for those trying to leave. At that time, Paul was living and working in Australia, travelling regularly to Thailand in an attempt to sponsor his wife's Australian visa. All was going well until a sweeping crackdown revealed that the immigration agent they were using to get her Thai visas; was arrested for fake visas. Along with many Burmese, she found herself a victim of a fraudster making money out of their desperate situation by faking visa stamps. At the time he happened to have Thida's passport in his possession so she was arrested for having a false visa and her passport was confiscated. Ironically two of the five visas she had in her passport were found to be real but the other three; all fake.

Paul eventually managed to raise the funds to pay her bail to release her, and their newborn baby, out of prison. Thida's court case was pending and Paul had to leave Thailand to earn money. In the mean time, fortunately, the Australian Embassy had approved her spouse visa and recognised their baby as an Australian citizen by descent. But, while the Australian embassy were happy to give Thida and her baby an entry visa into Australia, they could not help her leave Thailand. So, without her passport and a valid visa, Thida was stuck in an immigration nightmare in Bangkok.

Looking back, I cannot believe I had the guts to conjure up and execute her escape plan. And knowing what I know now, I'm not sure I would risk it again. Nevertheless, with a combination of naive optimism and confidence that the Australian Government would do the right thing, I found the courage.

The dilemma we were faced with was this: people from Central and South East Asian countries found in Thailand without a valid visa, were sent to immigration detention to serve a certain amount of time in prison for every day overstayed. They were then deported back to their home countries. People from wealthy nations were charged an amount per day overstayed, then free to leave. My grand plan was to try try for the latter. The calculated risk was that immigration detention with her Australian child might await her. The hope was that Thida would be taken to the airport.

So, I finally got the police to arrest her – which was necessary to satisfy their rules. After some money changed hands she was to be driven on the same day to the airport to fly to Australia. My Burmese activist friends advised me not to let her out of my sight in the hope that it would protect her from the abuses many Burmese suffer while in detention. There was also the general feeling that, if I didn't travel with her, the police would take the money and just drive her to the Burmese border anyway (a commonplace occurrence).

As the faceless urban cityscape unfolded I began to notice signs that we were indeed headed for the airport. Yet I still dared not allow myself to feel relief. We were stopped a few more times by police and immigration. Finally, escorted by six Immigration Police officers and a thousand staring eyes, we were on the Qantas flight. We sat back in our seats and both burst into tears. We had made it! During the flight two American backpackers came and complained about how much they had paid because they had overstayed their tourist visas by 40 days. I felt a sting of injustice and irony at the fact that Thida's husband and our charity had paid at least six times that amount for her freedom. These folks were simply enjoying a holiday travelling around the world without reading the rules.

Thida now lives happily with her husband and three children in Sydney Australia – and Aiden can't remember how he helped to save the day!

Chapter 1 – Love and Marriage

I was born in Mornington, a small seaside town in Melbourne, Australia. My parents were Dutch migrants which makes me, and most of my siblings, true-blue first generation Australians. I was 18 when the last amazing brother was added to our family. Mum and Dad adopted him when he was 16 after I brought him home from a refuge I was volunteering at and he made our family complete.

As a teenager I was awkward and very tall. Desperate not to stand out I worked extra hard perfecting a real Aussie accent. We lived in a council housing estate; which certainly helped with that. I took to some of the rougher Aussie phrases and slang like a duck to water. I also took to some of the lifestyle choices. And that is ultimately, what led me to spirituality. A social worker suggested to my parents that a Christian summer camp 'might be a good idea' to help with some of the bad choices.

In the summertime our family would often go on camping holidays (something I never now do by choice). My parents used to laugh that, even before the tent was even set up, I had the whole campsite sussed out. I would come back and regale them with tales of who had what at their tent site; and where everyone was from. They thought I was destined to be a news reporter. Instead, as it turned out, my busybody skills were to come in very handy in many years of community work.

Mornington is a sleepy, beachside kind of place. But from a young age I recall dreaming of a big bustling city. A place with buzz and stimulation. I wouldn't even have known to call it 'a city' back then – all I knew was – I wanted to be near the action. Where the people were. And – as soon as I could – I moved up to the city for Bible College and then University. Even back then, I had a sense I had lots to do and (fortunately) I seemed to have boundless energy to do it. Boredom was never an option and when I met my husband Ash, I had four part-time jobs at the same time.

I was just 19. He was at the same Christian youth workers' conference. I was instantly struck by the hot guy with a chequerboard hairdo and blonde tips. He wore a cool leather jacket and skinny little neck tie. It was the 80s after all. He was also a professional footballer (soccer player) – paid $50 per week to play! Of course, it was his charismatic personality that really attracted me – I'm not that shallow!

After a whirlwind romance we decided to join forces to on this adventure called life and married one year later. After the wedding we lived in a little suburb called Dingley Village. It was quite posh. Only a 5-minute drive, yet a world away, from the working class suburb of Springvale where many refugees and asylum seekers had started arriving and making their home.

Ash was working for a Christian youth organisation while completing his Bachelor's Degree in Theology. I was doing a teaching degree and working part time at a nursing home. We both imagined we would travel as missionaries one day. Ash fancied China and I wanted to go to Haiti. Back when we were young we thought we were in control of our lives and plans! And – although over the past 30 years we have lived as missionaries in three different urban neighbourhoods: 13 years in Springvale, Australia, 12 years in Klong Toey (a large slum in Bangkok), Thailand and now 7 years in Winson Green, England – never in China or Haiti.

Chapter 2 – Trial by Fire

Springvale, 1990

It's 3am and the incessant noise of 20 Teenagers is echoing in my head. I can smell acrid smoke from a sofa that's been slowly burning in the yard for the past two days. My eyelids are threatening to close but anxious adrenaline keeps me awake and alert in case trouble kicks off again. Tonight, so far, we have already had a very angry parent show up and drag their child back home. She snuck out of her bedroom window to come and meet her boyfriend. We were happy to be providing a safe place because we know a 14year old girl is better off here than hanging out on the streets of Springvale in the middle of the night.

Run-down and dilapidated, the building was given to our Christian Youth organisation by the Council. They figured, at least it would stop the local kids vandalising it. They also needed to address the complaints of general antisocial behaviour from residents of nearby Dingley Village. Large groups of teenagers had been gathering on the streets at night. We were barely adults ourselves – just 20years old – but full of naive optimism and silly enough to take the challenge on single-handedly. The main gang activity was happening at night so it made sense to run our youth drop-in sessions from 8pm – 3am, Thursday to Sunday. The place was already wrecked so we made an amateur graffiti mural on the wall and opened the place up for kids to hang out with us. We prayed the rival '3174' (postcode gang) boys wouldn't turn up looking for a fight.

I was a part way through university and Ash was also studying on top of his full time nocturnal role as a youth worker. But we were fired up. We started to see a side of life that our relatively privileged upbringings had protected us from. These young people had endured traumas and experienced barriers we could never truly understand. Addiction and mental illness was the result. For many of them, things at home were so difficult that the other kids at our drop-in centre became their family. Ash and I, on the other hand, rented a lovely new three-bedroom house five minutes down the road in the 'posh part of town' from his parents. We were on track with our career plans and life goals and the world was working out nicely for us. But these young people, their tragic stories and difficult unfair lives, was starting to mess with our sense of satisfaction. The rose-coloured glasses we had worn our whole lives were starting to fade and scratch. We were struck by the growing sensation that surely someone should do something more for these kids and their families.

A colleague of Ash's at the Christian Youth charity was working in the women's prison. They mentioned that when the women were released they often had nowhere to live. So we decided to take them into our home. We had three bedrooms after all! At the same time, as part of his job, Ash was regularly visiting the youth detention centre. Stories the women ex-prisoners told us about their teenage years revealed to us the downward spiral. It was apparent that the youths at the detention centre were on a one-track path to prison. If something was not done in time the kids would enter the same vicious cycle. We realised someone had to intervene and quick! But who?

That was a question I couldn't ignore: "If not you – then who?".

A few months after opening the drop-in centre, a local charity asked us to take in a teenage boy called Ishmael (name changed). He was 17 and still (only just) in school. He spoke very little about his mother. But from what we could gather she had been an addict before she passed away. After she died he went to live with his elderly grandparents. They were amazing, loving people, but as their health began to fail, the day-to-day stresses of raising a teenage boy soon became too much for them.

We were becoming foster parents and it took some getting used to. Particularly because Ishmael loved death metal music. What sounded, to us, like vomiting cats was often heard caterwauling from his room. He took up kick boxing, and I still remember the pride we felt at one of his fights, sitting in the stadium, as they announced the fighters. The first boy came out to rousing Rocky music. Then came Ishmael and his tortured animal tunes. He bounced about and punched the air.

Our other foster son, 11-year-old Metus was with us too and we all cheered along as the fight got underway. A few kicks and then a big punch to the head and his opponent was down on the floor. We rose to our feet celebrating and clapping before it dawned on us that the other boy was unconscious. A medic and ambulance were called. Sitting down sheepishly we also noticed the family sitting next to us start to cry and we realised Ishmael had knocked out their son. It was at this exact moment I became a pacifist.

Our youth drop-in centre was becoming quite successful and was busy every night. Ash was later honoured with 'Junior Citizen of the Year Award' in recognition of the impact of that early work. But it's true to say we were on a very steep learning curve. We had no idea what we were doing. Literally – just 'giving it a go'. Our naivety was highlighted when the Christian Youth charity head office received a phone bill in their name from the drop-in centre for a whopping AUS$1200. Mostly incurred by listed calls to dial-up sex lines. Teenagers – you gotta' love 'em! While the programme appeared to be a success, the hours were killing us. We both had day jobs and study commitments. We were burning through volunteers who found it all too much. However, we were connecting to the community by making headway with families in need. So, we felt we couldn't possibly consider stopping. Or even slowing down. We were sleepwalking through the day but buzzing with anxious energy all night.

One day while we were out, Ishmael, broke into the youth building with his girlfriend. He fell asleep while smoking and the sofa burst into flames. Miraculously, they made it out with only singed hair. The building wasn't so lucky and the only thing salvageable was a smoke damaged TV that had also been soaked by the firefighters' hose. I would like to say that we were devastated. That was certainly the face we were showing to the remaining fire crews and local council inspector. But the truth is, Ash and I looked at each other and said a silent, "Thank you, God!" This was going to give us our first weekend of normal sleep in months. Still dazed, we loaded the soggy TV into the back of our car and made our way home. We hit a bump in the road making the tailgate of the car fall open and the TV landed on the street. We loaded it back up and dragged ourselves home. We plugged the waterlogged, smoked filled and dented TV into the electric socket and couldn't believe that it worked perfectly! If you ever see an appliance with the brand name 'Blackstripe' – buy it!

Unlike that TV, Ash and I were not invincible. We escaped to our friend's countryside caravan with the intention of getting some thinking space. Suddenly the backlog of exhaustion caught up with us. Our eyelids refused to stay open and on the three-hour-drive we had to pull over four times to sleep. When we eventually made it to the caravan park we slept two days straight. I couldn't even will myself to go and pee in the public toilets. I found a fortuitous plastic box under the bed and 'made do'. By day three I finally felt ready to face the world again and mustered enough energy to get up. As my feet hit the floor, I looked down and realised, much to my dismay, that my makeshift toilet was actually the container for the family's toothbrushes. Hunting down a lookalike replacements in the local shops was not what I had planned for the first day of our new chapter! But at least it motivated me to emerge from hibernation with renewed sense of purpose as I tried to cover up the evidence of my actions.

In more ways than one, the fire at the neighbourhood youth club was a blessing in disguise. It forced us to think less about running projects and programmes and more about finding an organic way of serving young people. One that looked more like a big, extended, messy family (which is more often than not what they were missing). Being youth workers without a youth centre meant the contact had to happen in our own home. We learnt that sharing our own place created space – not only for deep transformation for the people of the community we welcomed – but also within us. Our next-door neighbours, however, did not exactly thank us!

You don't expect to take on parenting teenagers in your early twenties. But that is what was happening. We realised that, for many of these young people, the chaos they were acting out started years ago when they were kids in struggling homes. We could comprehend their adolescent behaviour by understanding the abuse they suffered in their early lives. The realisation that we were becoming like family to these young people was brought home to us one Sunday afternoon. It was a Sunday like any other when we received the phone call from a group of girls crying in the toilets of Hungry Jacks (the Aussie version of Burger King). They were hysterical. Sobbing and panicking down the line, I eventually worked out that a young girl called Renae, had fallen off the back of Anton's illegally ridden motorbike and had slid across the road on her face. The kids were too scared to call an ambulance; so they called us instead. I drove down there and found what looked like a massacre in the toilets. Blood everywhere and what appeared to be her nose between her eyes. The girls were crying uncontrollably and the boys had taken themselves, and the offending motorbike, to our house where Ash had to deal with it – and them.

I drove Renae and her hysterical friends to the hospital where she was rushed through to A&E leaving the crying girls in the waiting room. I had the awful job of calling Rene's parents. Within the hour they had prepped her for surgery, which involved scrubbing her face with a firm scrubbing brush to make sure the gravel was out to reduce the chances of scarring.

When the furious parents arrived, Ash found himself standing between the trembling young Anton and Renae's livid father – trying to stop him getting pummelled. I hid behind the hysterical girls who were still in floods of tears. I've never been brave when faced with conflict. No amount of teacher training or theological theories can equip you for these moments. Ash, at that time, was training as a minister, but Bible College definitely didn't offer any classes to prepare him for situations like this. A few years later, I realised that a teaching degree really wasn't right for me, so I switched to social work instead. I desperately hoped it would better equip me for the many more chaotic moments to come. Sadly, it didn't. Our twenty-something selves did not have all the right answers. We just muddled along with our best guesses, hoping not to make too much of a mess.

The last 30 years have really just been one out-of-my-depth experience after another. I have had to cling to my belief in a God who shows up when the shit hits the fan.

Unbelievably – as I am writing this story down thinking I will have to change Renae's real name (I had no way of contacting her to ask permission after three decades) this very night she has contacted me completely of-the-blue on Facebook!

"Hi Anji, I am not sure if you remember me. I was a very lost young girl many moons ago (around 1989) these things may help you remember me – my name was Renae ... I was homeless, you gave me a bed at the Dingley community house, I was in a horrific motorbike accident, you took me to a youth camp in Belgrave (I still have the bible you gave me) I spent a lot of time with you at the Dingley church, I did my work experience with you in the field of welfare work, I also remember going to a party with you down Rosebud way? I suffered with a lot of trauma as a child and my youth years were chaotic and messy. I have blocked a lot of things out of my life from my younger years. I have been waking with memories of a few things lately and you and Ash have been in those memories. The memories I have of you and Ash are positive and calming and I am seeing more how much you did for me. I am reaching out now to say thank you. Thank you for all the love, support & guidance you gave me as a young person. I am not sure when we parted ways. I went on to live a life of self harm and destruction but always wanting to be the best person I could be. I am now 45 years old, have 2 beautiful daughters, have my own successful business, own my home in the ... and have a wonderful supportive, loving husband. I also became a youth worker and alcohol & drug worker around 15 years ago as I wanted to give back and help other young people just as you and Ash did for me. I woke this morning thinking of you, your names were unclear and then I started to remember you. When I googled you I still wasn't 100% sure until I listened to a clip of you on the internet and then I heard your voice and knew for certain it is you. I felt the need to reach out. I want you

to know I am grateful for all that you did for me, you never gave up. You truly are an inspiration, a pure white light and an angel walking this earth. Thank you from the bottom of my heart"

I guess this eerily-timed message showed me that, even when we didn't have a clue what we were doing, somehow God was able to turn it into something good. To know that we had a positive impact on the life of someone else is such a privilege and a buzz!

Chapter 3 – Lessons Learned in a Slum

Klong Toey, 2002

Sweat is dripping down my face. The stink of disinfectant hangs off every atom in the humid air. Row after row in front of me all I can see are disfigured emaciated bodies. I had fancied myself as a bit of a modern-day Mother Theresa when I signed up to volunteer at the AIDS hospice. But I quickly realised I'm really not that nice. I'm counting down the minutes until the day finally ends.

We have relocated to live in Klong Toey, Thailand's biggest slum with our five-year-old daughter, Amy in tow. Ash and I spend our mornings learning Thai at a language school in one of Bangkok's busy shopping districts. I then spend my afternoons helping out at the hospice. By now, I have had some years of experience living and serving as a qualified social worker in a poor community in Australia. I'm confident that I can make a positive contribution to this community. But my conviction is rapidly diminishing. Firstly, I have no ability to communicate and secondly, a complete stranger to the local ways. I feel lost to say the least. However, I remain determined to tackle the injustice I see amongst the poorest of the poor. But I don't even know how to order dinner.

Many in the hospice are dying of AIDS because they were sex workers in an effort to overcome poverty. Or because of intravenous drugs used in the effort to numb the pain of poverty. I have never trained as a nurse, but my role as a Mum to our daughter – as well as the many foster kids we cared for – has given me plenty of practice changing nappies. So, at the AIDS hospice that is the role I am given: changing adult diapers, colostomy bags and massaging the patients' aching limbs as they waste away. There is little anyone can really do for them by the time they reach the hospice. I feel utterly helpless as I can't speak Thai and am unable to even say kind words of comfort. So I do what I can – apply creams, ointments and provide gentle human touch as they wait to slowly die. In 2003, when anti-Retroviral (ARV) drugs are finally made available to the poor, those lucky enough to receive them no longer needed to go to the AIDS hospice to die. And, although home-based care sounds like a great alternative in wealthier countries, when your home is an overcrowded searing hot tin shack; prolonged life is almost crueller.

My efforts at Thai language school each morning seem to be getting me nowhere fast. The neighbours are forever giggling at my Thai pronunciation and smirking at my alien gesticulations. One day our daughter Amy turns to me and says: "Mum, I thought we came here to help the Thai people, but they are helping us way more". She is right of course. It is extremely humbling to unexpectedly be the student and certainly takes the shine off my grandiose delusions of 'saving the world'. I am clueless but keen to learn. Father Richard Rohr, a great mentor of ours over the years, talks about 'praying for a daily humiliation to keep the ego in check'. During my time in Klong Toey, peppered with embarrassment and humiliation, I think my daily quota is full for the rest of my life. The full extent of my understanding of it grew slowly in direct proportion to my language skills.

Now, looking back, I remember days permeated with a heavy sense of failure and futility. Even when I wasn't getting things wrong, my efforts made little difference. People were dying and I couldn't do anything about it. For some reason, maybe just sheer bloody mindedness, I continued to volunteer at the AIDS hospice for two years. Right up until when my son, Aiden was born. Although I constantly questioned whether I was making any difference, at the same time I was learning that self-esteem can't come from doing things that look good to the outside world. I discovered that self-worth is built by living life authentically. Living in line with what you believe. By remembering I am enough in God's eyes no matter what I do. I say this with the benefit of hindsight. But at the time I just felt constantly bewildered – yet driven by a sense that I was 'supposed' to be there. There was a little whisper of hope that I believe was, perhaps, the gentle voice of God.

Another of the many lessons I learnt in the slums of Klong Toey was that my scientific or 'rational' Western worldview, that I assumed was the 'right one', was not as sensible as I was raised to believe. Conversely in fact much of what initially seemed crazy and weird to me, in Thailand, was actually really quite sensible. An example of this was our little slum home. Two of the walls of the house were made from porous Besser bricks. Patterned holes at the top of the walls allowed every mosquito and cockroach in Klong Toey to come in and make themselves at home. The other walls, made of plywood and tin, were so thin and soggy that when we closed the front door for some desperately needed privacy, Amy's little friends would poke holes through the walls with sticks when they wanted her to come out to play. Initially we used plasticine to fill in these holes, but eventually gave up when the plasticine became a more significant portion of the wall than plywood. We realised the path of less resistance was to live with less privacy and keep the door open.

When Amy became seriously ill with dengue fever we realised something had to be done. So we stuffed the the holes in the bricks with plastic shopping bags. At first the plan went swimmingly; and we were relatively mosquito-free. However, after a few months passed the plastic bags seemed to take on a life of their own – literally. A community of local slum rats had found that plastic bags make perfect nests for baby rats. Suddenly we were more overrun with more critters than ever before. One day, lying in bed (aka: a mattress on the floor) a fat rat, on a mission for a tasty morsel of Phad Thai, had become so familiar with us humans in his bedroom that it ran straight across our bed towards the front door. I jumped up in utter horror and only just managed to freeze the scream in my throat so as not to wake Amy. Ash raced (faster than a hungry rat) outside to pick up one of the mangy stray slum cats – of which there are plenty. The hapless cat was more than happy to suddenly have found the purpose for which it was born. He chased the rat around the small room finally cornering it on our, suddenly popular, mattress. This was no shrinking-violet gutter rat. It promptly aimed a mighty fanged chomp right on the cat's face! The poor cat ran back out to the alley crying. Rat 1. Cat 0. Finally, it was Ash and a trusty broom that won the day. Needless to say, we didn't get much sleep that night.

The next day the plastic bags were ceremoniously discarded. Our next attempt at hole filling was in the form of pieces of plywood. We drilled them tightly into the bricks against the wily mosquitos. After a few days passed and once again we thought we had won the battle. That was until we noticed the terrible stink of raw sewage suddenly seemed to ooze from every pore of our small home. It began to dawn on us that the holey bricks were not an unintentional design flaw but perhaps part of an unspoken slum law: airflow is really important when your sewage is under the house. No less than 10 neighbours had stood and watched us drill in that plywood. Not one of them said a word! Years later I reminded them of that experience and they shamelessly laughed. With not a hint of remorse they said: "Yeah we all thought you were totally crazy. It gave us a great giggle!"

During the early years in Klong Toey, our family life was defined by reliance on an incredible woman named, 'Blah'. She was our next-door neighbour, and helped us so much. We sometimes wondered if she was listening to our conversations through the wall. One night we were lying in bed talking about how great it would be to get a bed throw. We were tired of sleeping in sheets covered in the dirty footprints of the neighbourhood kids who enjoyed climbing all over the bed during the day. To no avail we had hunted through the stalls of fresh vegetables, butchered animals, fruit and home appliances at Klong Toey market. (Tesco Supermarket would open in Klong Toey area a year later and make life so much easier). The next morning, Blah walked in with a big blue bed throw that she had somehow bought for us!

Another time, after Ash had been confiding in me how much he really missed toast, Blah showed up in the morning with a toaster and bread. She had so little herself. Yet she was, and remains, one of the most generous people we have ever known.

When sharing with a group of German students I had brought to Klong Toey, Blah told us how she came to be Christian in Buddhist Thailand. God appeared to her in a dream telling her that an angel would come and give her a bible. And that apparently, I was that angel! I vaguely remembered 17 years earlier, trying to communicate with Blah, in my three words of Thai and her broken English. I had thought she was asking me about church and whether we were Christians. In my sign language-y way, I picked up a bible and showed it to her. She took it with a big smile thinking I was giving it to her. I now realise what that transaction meant to her. Much deeper than for me at the time. Although Ash was pretty mad I gave away his precious leather-covered edition! Throughout the 12 years we were in Thailand, so much can be described that way: me thinking one thing was happening and then, years later, finding out something else entirely was actually going on (and understood by everyone else).

Now, seven years into life in Birmingham, UK, speaking the same mother tongue (mostly) and, compared to Thailand, more cultural similarity than you could shake a stick at: it is the same. I am only now starting to hear about the cultural *faux pas* I made in the early days. I have learnt that although Australians speak the same language and, superficially at least, share English culture (some might say 'lack of'), there are also profound differences. Luckily, I have really great teammates who are now more comfortable pointing out if I am being inappropriate or saying things that are easily misunderstood. They keep reminding me that *thongs* are called *flip flops* here and *pants* are not *trousers*. Subtle cultural differences so often cause misunderstandings and – worse – hurt feelings. It seems God enjoys allowing me to be an example. In recent years, feeling less insecure than when I was younger, I have become better at turning these embarrassments around and using them to open a group up into real conversation. I think it would have crushed me to know, or admit, some of these things – even five years ago. But now they somehow seem more like unexpected and unintentional gifts – like Ash's bible was to Blah.

Of course, Blah loves us. But she really loves Amy, and took her everywhere. Often alongside her two nieces, on countless trips and adventures. By taking Amy into her extended family, her Thai got really good and she even went to a Thai speaking pre-school with Blah's youngest niece, Bell. Every day for those first few months they played outside the front of our houses or at Blah's family shop. My mother-in-law remembers taking Amy on a shopping trip the first time she visited us in Bangkok. The taxi driver was struggling to understand where to go until little seven-year-old Amy piped up in perfect Thai, *"Gou ja by su kong ti Lotus.* We want to go shopping at Lotus please!"*. The poor driver was so confused. All he could see in the back seat was a little blond girl speaking Thai with a local – fairly impolite – dialect! I was slower to learn Thai than Amy; Blah would correct my tones all the time. A few years later I realised that the reason I was having so much trouble with my tones and accent was because Blah has a cleft pallet! So, I like to think, I was speaking Thai with a perfect cleft pallet tone.

Two years into life in Klong Toey we were getting ready to head back to Australia for a visit. Blah came up to me with a bracelet her sister had made, asking: "Can you sell these in Australia?" For years Blah's sister had been hiding in Blah's house rarely, if ever, venturing out. She owed money to a local loan shark and was too scared to go outside. She spent her time sitting on the floor threading phuang malai, Thai flower garlands, for her sons to sell in the streets. Their sweet jasmine smell makes them really popular in Thailand and they are hung as offerings in front of Buddha statues, pictures of holy people and monks. They are also hung on the rear view mirror of taxis – which is often a blessing for the clients! Nevertheless, her sister needed money badly and Blah thought we could help. And, she was right. Our friends in Australia paid more than we asked for the bracelets. I saw potential and took samples of designs popular in Australia and Europe back to Bangkok so Blah's sister could adjust her craft for a foreign market. (In Thailand, copyright means the right to copy). When I got home to Thailand, 'Klong Toey Handicrafts' was set up. Blah

15

helped at every step. This social enterprise really grew when we met the amazing Liz Maher who developed the business to the point where the turnover was AUS$280,000 and provided employment for at least 40 people in Klong Toey. You've never met a harder working volunteer than Liz, and she made me look like I was in slow motion!

Blah's drive to see this business set up came directly from her life story. She was desperate to help create a business so other women would not have to go through what she went through. It was after six months into our time in Thailand we found out Blah's real story. A Thai friend who spoke great English was out with us for dinner and Blah asked her to translate as she shared her life with us.

Blah was the eighth of sixteen children. When Blah was eight, her family lost everything in a house fire, all too common in the slums. Her mum was forced to borrow money. So much so, that the debt owed to loan sharks was impossible to pay back. The family couldn't afford to send the children to school and Blah tells of having just one pair of shoes that had to be shared around the family. As often happens in large, poor families, she was married off very young. Her husband was a brute and mistreated her from day one. One day her sister said: "Even a dog is treated better. Leave him and come to live with me!" Blah's marriage had brought no relief, so Blah still felt great pressure to help the family out of debt. It's often the case in Thailand that the daughters are responsible for the family financially and the sons are responsible for the spiritual wellbeing. Most young Thai men become monks for either a short or long periods in their lives and therefore bring the family good karma and spiritual protection. That's when Blah's friend suggested she could earn good money as a sex worker in Hong Kong. Blah accepted this as the only way to help her family and for her younger siblings to go to school. She was soon trafficked to Hong Kong. Unfortunately, the plan quickly turned into a nightmare and the promised money never materialised. The people she worked for took her passport and locked her in a room the size of a cupboard where she was forced to service around ten men a day. Eventually, a customer took pity on her and helped her escape. She was free, but without money or passport and not speaking the language. She was soon arrested and eventually deported back to Thailand. The sordid details of what she went through are not my story to share. But the result is that Blah could never have her own children. And in a country like Thailand with no social security, and no care system, this means real poverty and destitution in old age.

Despite the horror of what happened to her, Blah is a loving and generous person. Although the trauma is always just below the surface. I wish I could say that she never had to return to sex work but that would not be true. The extreme poverty, low wages and terrible work conditions in the squid factory where she had a 'real job' made sex work the only viable option if the family were to get out of their crushing debt.

Taking a huge risk, Blah went overseas again. But this time it was to another country where she faired a bit better. Her dream, like many Thai girls, was to marry a foreigner who would support her and her family. Sadly, for Blah, the man who became her second husband was actually registered bankrupt and therefore unable to sponsor her to live with him. In the early days of our time there, he would send for her about three times a year to visit him and occasionally visited Thailand. The money she continued to earn from him – and other sex work – was eventually enough to raise the family out of extreme poverty. They were able to own a few slum dwellings which they rented out (one to us) which brought in some income. They also had a shop at the front of their house and the younger siblings and nephews and nieces were all able to go to school. In those early days Blah would disappear from the slum for periods of time. When she came back she immediately took Amy out to nice places and buy her things. When we understood her story, we were humbled and embarrassed to realise that she was spending some of her hard-earned money on our daughter. This brought both of them great joy and Ash and I a kind of tortured, horrified gratitude. But as Blah got older this work involved taking huge risks and she suffered violence and abuse.

17

Soon Amy also came to understand how Blah survived and this seemed to make her love and admire her more.

Today, 'Klong Toey Handicrafts' has been re-branded as 'Roy-rak Jewellery' (https://www.royrakbeadinglove.org/). You can buy stunning goods made by Blah and the women of Klong Toey and when you do, you will be giving these women an income which, for many of them, is a real pathway to hope.

Chapter 4 – Hijab, Hatred and Hunger

Winson Green, 2015

If I'm honest, I'm feeling nervous and a little bit scared. It feels strange to be wearing this double-layered headscarf (hijab) ensemble and, even with my blonde hair tucked away, I wonder if I look at all convincing. I'm terrified of doing something that causes offence and of how people will treat me wearing a headscarf. Trying to cover my hand tattoos I realise that, as usual, I haven't really thought this through!

We first arrived in Birmingham shortly before the Charlie Hebdo Islamic extremist terror attack in Paris. We had already made many new Muslim friends when the awful news broke. Then, as Islamophobia began to sweep through the UK, I became increasingly aware of the terrible abuse some of my hijab wearing neighbours were facing. They were easy targets. One day after the Paris attacks, my friend came to me crying, holding her 6-year-old son's hand. She had been spat upon on the bus, called vile names and told to 'go back home' (despite having been born and raised in the UK). All of this happened in front of her frightened son while everyone else sat by and did nothing. That, I think, is what upset her the most. She was on a bus full of people and no one said or did anything to help her.

I felt so helpless. All I could do was wash the spit from her headscarf and make her a clumsy cup of tea. I felt wrong, guilty and somehow complicit. I know I wouldn't have got involved either as the ignorant guy sounded terrifying. I remember thinking: what can I do? What, if anything, should my response as a Christian be? Someone should do something about this!

So I decided to highlight the issue. The least I could do was to walk in the shoes of my friend – and write about it. I decided to wear a hijab for ten days and then share my experiences online. Not for 'cultural appropriation' but to show solidarity and raise awareness of the horrendous racism that Muslim women were suffering daily in my community.

I was stunned and shaken by the deliberate intimidation I faced on public transport (particularly in central London). Walking down the street in broad daylight – minding my business – I was called horrible names. On the other hand, I was heartened by the friendliness of local women who excitedly gave me instructions and sent me helpful YouTube clips on how to properly tie my scarf. I found that people in Birmingham city centre were a lot friendlier to me. Kind Muslim men helped pick up my dropped shopping, or gave me directions when I was clearly lost trying to work out directions on my phone (3G back then!). So much of what I had perceived as stand-offish by some sections of the community I now realised was fear of the abuse that they have come to expect from white British people in this newly tense political environment. I also realised that, just as there is such a thing as a bad hair day, there are also bad headscarf days!

Adam Hills, an Australian comedian who has become well known in the UK and has a weekly show called *The Last Leg* on Channel 4. During this period, he came out in support of the Muslim community and against Islamophobia. This caused his social media to go wild with comments. I added a comment and linked it to my online 10-day hijab journey blog. This resulted in hundreds of extremely negative remarks aimed directly at me. The thing that still shocks me to this day is the hate, vitriol and even death threats that came from so-called Christians. Regardless of what brand of Christian you profess to be, surely hate of this magnitude is not compatible with any idea of a loving God?

The Bible is full of unlikely heroes from foreign lands. Gentiles (non-Jewish people) play a starring role in stories about Jesus' life. And it remains true that people on the outside of society's 'norms' are often more willing to care for other people. They share similar struggles and can empathise with the pain of exclusion. I am proud to partner with many Muslim friends on projects including our cooking school social enterprise, *Flavours of Winson Green*, organising community Iftar meals. People of all faiths eat together in our back garden during Ramadan. Our

Muslim neighbours have taught me so much about out-gracing prejudice. They are invaluable local assets and star players in making our neighbourhood become the best it can be. I get to see God's love shining through them as we work together as equal partners towards our mutual mission to transform the community we all live in.

The *Flavours of Winson Green* catering social enterprise is a great example of transferable learning. Back in Klong Toey, we supported our friend and neighbour Poo (short for Chompoo) to start her own Thai cooking school social enterprise www.cookingwithpoo.com. She has become hugely successful and her cookbook cheekily called *Cooking with Poo* won the Frankfurt Book Fair 'World's Oddest Book Title' Award in 2011. Having a bit of fun with her name was a deliberate act to draw free advertising and create some laughter in an often all too sad world. Her school was the number one Bangkok tourist attraction on TripAdvisor for a long time. She was even invited to do a YouTube cooking session with the world-renowned chef Jamie Oliver. Still today, Poo continues to use her cooking gift as a means to employ other local women in the Klong Toey Slum. Her amazing story – of her rise from poverty to become a successful entrepreneur – can be found on her website.

Although Birmingham is another planet compared to Thailand, I found that the same business model worked within my new life and new context too. Cooking requires little spoken English and celebrates the skills and cultural heritage of women who have spent hours grafting away in their kitchens. Women who often struggle to access employment opportunities in the workplace. Our mobile cooking courses give migrant women a platform to teach their incredible recipes to white British people. The *Flavours of Winson Green* social enterprise was born out of a desire to also help non-Muslim people meet and get to know Muslim women as people just like them: mothers, teachers, cooks and women with stories. It also serves as a way to create friendships across cultural, ethnic and religious divides. It has successfully been all this and so much more over the past four years. We have had women join

Flavours from as far-flung as Yemen, Afghanistan, Mauritius, Gambia, Ghana, Slovakia, Pakistan, Philippines, Senegal and Somalia to name a few. It is a constant privilege and honour to learn from and hear the remarkable life-stories these women have endured – and survived. We should be so proud that they now call Britain their home. I may not have much money in the bank, but I feel incredibly rich and have the most privileged life because of these diverse friends.

The irony that I am somehow at the heart of culinary social enterprises is not lost on those who know me best. Of course food is a universal social glue and sharing meals together is a common thread that binds all relationships. I mentioned earlier that when I was young I trained as a teacher. But something that is not so commonly known is that I was training as a Home Economics and English teacher. Those who have lived under my roof will literally will laugh out loud to read this because I am probably the world's worst cook. I am known worldwide as the one who burns everything. Indeed, 'Charcoal Chips' is one of my nicknames. In Birmingham, I came scarily close to burning the house down after putting spaghetti sauce on and then going to work for 5 hours! In the early days of married life in Australia I completely burned the bottom of a pot right through until nothing remained but a glowing red ember. The smell was horrendous and the bill for replacing all the curtains in the lounge was even worse as it never came out. I wish I could say that I learnt my lesson, but I am guilty of being a serial pot killer time and again. My son even started sharing Instagram pictures with his friends of his daily burnt offering breakfasts.

In Thailand my reputation took on a particular significance. I was known not just as a bad cook – but also a weird one. For a start we had no kitchen – so that was a challenge. Every now and then I would fancy some non-Asian food. Nowadays, it is really easy to get Western food in Bangkok. But 18 years ago it was not so readily available. So, one day when I was pregnant with our son Aiden I went to the posh foreign supermarket where I spent half our weekly budget on a box of American muesli, and an even bigger fortune on buying ingredients for nachos. I was very strict in those first few years, desperate not to standout, so I wouldn't let Ash buy anything that I had decided Thai people in the slum didn't have. So, it was only as I got inside our one-room house that I remembered we had no oven or grill to melt the cheese! I did however have an excellent hair dryer. He often complained about the fact that we only had two mugs and three plates, but my hairdryer was worth $100! Well – it turned out to be worth its weight in gold that day. It was just the thing I needed to make nachos without a grill or oven. A few nachos were sacrificed as I adjusted the settings to be hot enough to melt the cheese but not so strong as to blow the corn chips across the room. A number of the Thai ladies had gathered around to watch me cook, and I could understand enough Thai by then to know they were commenting on how foreigners also use the hair dryer for cooking and how strange that was. I didn't have enough Thai to explain properly that I wasn't your typical foreigner. A few years later I took up the challenge to see what other household appliances could be repurposed for making food and managed to perfect a fairly decent cheese-toastie with a clothes iron! Even last week I was shown how to make the perfect toasted cheese sandwich using our charity's blacksmithing forge!

In Birmingham, we have been seriously shocked by the simultaneous prevalence of food waste in the face of real hunger. It makes absolutely no sense that companies dump so much perfectly edible surplus stock; while kids go hungry at home. As a result, we do weekly food collections and use what would have been thrown out by shops to feed up to 50 people twice-weekly at free community meals in our home. We have partnered with Starbucks, Prét a Manger and Gregg's just to name a few. We have also linked up with a brilliant initiative called Real Junk Food. (https://www.trjfpcentral.co.uk) Their tag line is: *"Food is for bellies not bins"*. They redistribute leftover food by running 'Pay as You Feel' cafés that cook meals from ingredients that would otherwise be thrown away. Customers pay whatever they are able to, or help wash dishes etc. It's a dignified way to deal with food poverty as well as a great environmental initiative. Wasted food was never an issue in Bangkok as little food shops throughout the slum would use the unsold food to feed their families while buying fresh supplies each day for the customers. This meant for us we never got sick from street food in the slum as it was made fresh daily. We only ever got sick from posh hotels and restaurants who tended to buy in bigger amounts and keep their leftovers for longer. Ironic really!

In all three countries we have been based in, food has proven to be the best way to build bridges and bring people together. Perhaps that's why Jesus asked us to remember him during a simple meal with diverse friends.

Chapter 5 – Lost in Translation

Perth Airport, 2007

Standing in customs control, face flushed with embarrassment, desperately hoping that I'm not going to be in trouble. It seems to be a theme with me. I hadn't thought it through! The wooden items packed into my Australia-bound suitcase had to be declared and now I am going through the humiliation of having giant wooden penises, that hold special meaning for Thai people, inspected. Amy is giving me evil looks in between messing around with the clip on her all pink bag and hat ensemble. Ash is trying to pretend he is not with me and I can feel my face burning up.

I was travelling back to Australia to speak at a theological college on the topic: "Challenges when working amongst people of other religions and superstitions". Teacher Training had taught me that visual aids are a great way to engage students, particularly non-academic ones, like myself. I was keen to highlight the unconscious bias in the subject. It makes me cringe how easily we notice weird things in someone else's culture while being totally oblivious to the superstitions that we ourselves live by. I thought bringing Thai Balakiks (phallus statues- big wooden penises to be exact!) would be an icebreaker to get the students talking. I think Western Christians believe some strange things that onlookers find bizarre, and I was keen to unpack how that influences our ability to work with others.

If you've ever watched the TV show *Nothing to Declare* you will know that Australia has some of the strictest border controls in the world. All items made from natural fibre, along with wood and any kind of food, is strictly forbidden. I hadn't registered that I was going to have to hand these wooden phallic statues over for inspection! My husband and kids were mortified when they realised we would all need to go through the 'Items to Declare' section together (as is the rule for families travelling together). As I handed these two large wooden penises to the border control officer I said, "It's not what it looks like!" He responded with, "Yeah sure. They are for the ladies in the office, right? I've heard it all before." So I told him, "No, I'm a missionary and these are for a lecture I'm giving at a church college." Without taking a breath he wryly replied: "Can I join your church?". After show and tell with his colleagues and a bit more hilarity, the officer took them to be sprayed for bugs and we were finally on our way. It took a long time for my family to forgive me for the embarrassment, but they were always braced for public humiliation, having to live with me.

In preparation for the lecture, I had spent the previous few weeks asking Thais about what these phallic objects meant. Of the 25 people asked, I received 23 different explanations. I realised yet again that I still functioned with a black and white world-view while living in a country that had a much more free-flowing and fluid way of seeing reality. A friend, who drove taxis wore a little wooden penis on his belt. For him it was a way to ward off dog bites when walking home through the slum late at night. The attacks could be savage. Our foster son had one hanging around his waist to fend off illness as he had been a sickly baby. Two ladies who sold food at the fresh market believed theirs helped boost profits. I have a faded memory of a time when, new to Thailand, I bought socks for my daughter and watched in confusion as the sales assistant waved a big wooden penis over the products before handing them to me. At the time I was too mortified to ask why. But now it made more sense! Another shopkeeper had a large tree made of porcelain penis branches that he believed brought in new customers. A bit like the Chinese Cat with the waving arm. Another neighbour wore a penis talisman on his key ring to help his virility.

As the wooden phalluses passed around the classroom, the group readily engaged in a discussion about different world-views and ways of seeing faith. I explained that Thailand is like a beautiful impressionist painting. The reasons behind rituals are subjective and varied. They are less bothered by standardised scientific answers and much more open to mysticism. You wouldn't go to a gallery and ask why that particular line is placed at a specific angle. You just appreciate the way the whole picture comes together and moves you. I've found this is a really helpful perspective that allows me to have a more holistic practice of Faith.

The great thing about living in different cultures is learning to appreciate very different ways of seeing the world. Even when illumination is greatly over-shadowed by utter confusion. I have felt chronically baffled in all the places we have lived but never more so than in Thailand.

The first of countless examples is the night I was called to attend to a family whose disabled daughter had died suddenly in the night. She was laying on a mat on the floor of the dark hot slum shack. Next to her, on a roughly constructed platform, that could barely be described as a bed, laid her 68-year-old grandfather who, having suffered a stroke some years earlier, was unable to walk. There was really nothing I could do to comfort this family. Particularly as I was aware of the horrible abuse this young girl had received at their hands. Secretly, as awful as it sounds, I was relieved – for her – that her torturous life was over. Uncomfortable with my helplessness, I asked what they needed and was asked for a mosquito net. I dashed home and brought one back only to find everyone had left the hut. Trying to get sense out of granddad was useless because his speech was affected by the stroke. So I hung up the net and was tucking it in around him as the family arrived back to the house, trying not to step on the body of his granddaughter laying on the floor. I was stuck by a strange silence and odd looks from the family. This wasn't unusual as Thais are generally very polite with their silence. It was normal not to be told I had done something wrong. I returned home and there soon came a knock on the wall from a less polite neighbour. She was laughing her head off and calling me names. The mosquito net was to cover the deceased girl to stop the cats (of which the house had many) crossing over the body and bringing bad luck! I assumed they wanted to protect their living relative from mosquito-borne dengue fever. It did strike me as sadly ironic that this girl was probably treated better after she died than while she was living.

But yet I felt my feeble attempts to help had just made things more awkward for the family.

Another more light-hearted example of misunderstanding the culture came a few months later. *Cooking with Poo* had become such a success that Poo needed to employ staff to help with her ever-growing customer base. This is a complex thing to do in a crowded slum community where there are difficult and complicated histories between families. Many of the people she was expected to hire; would have simply been unable to do the job. As I had recently moved into a new section of the slum which, despite being only 500 metres away from the previous section, had a completely different community, it was decided that I should look for someone to work with Poo there.

I had noticed a woman called Noi. I walked past her a few times a day from my house. She was always hard at work either selling food or helping her various nieces and nephews with homework. She wasn't too shy to say hello to me and have a chat and this would be a great quality to have working with foreign customers. I wanted to ask her to join Poo's enterprise. But, by this stage, I had learnt that in Thai culture, when asked a direct question, Thai people feel like they have to say 'yes', even if they want to say 'no'! I believe she would have felt even added pressure to accept as we had started a weekly kids club that her daughter and nephews attended. This concept has a specific word in Thai, *grengjaiy*. It doesn't have an English translation deep and all-encompassing enough to translate. In a very limited way *grengjaiy* means to be 'indebted' or 'beholden'. If I were to ask if Noi wanted to work for the cooking school, I was worried she would feel *grengjaiy* and say yes … even if she didn't want to. So instead, I cleverly explained to her all about the school. I told her how busy it was and how Poo really needed staff. I then asked her – would she like to take a look? She said yes. As far as I was aware Noi was 'choosing' to work with Poo every day after that. A bit later I asked Poo if she was any good and Poo answered 'yes'. It wasn't until a full 12 months later I heard about the confusion I had caused. Apparently, when I sent Noi to have a look, that is exactly what she did. For about three weeks – she just sat and looked! Poo thought it was strange that Noi came to work and didn't work, but because I had recommended her and because of this concept of *grengjaiy* she would have to accept Noi as part of her team. Noi also thought it was strange that I told her to just go and watch, as she saw how busy Poo was and felt like she should be helping. Eventually Noi asked Poo if she'd like some help and much to Poo's relief, she proved to be a quick and hard worker who is still Poo's second in command to this day.

A year later, as the business continued to expand, I sent another young woman to 'have a look'. Noi and Poo discussed it among themselves and guessed that I might have asked her to watch. "Yes", she said, and they laughed and said: "We would actually like you to work." I was mortified when I found out what I'd done! I really thought I had mastered the Thai language by that stage. It's one thing to speak the words, it's another to grasp how they will be heard!

Although these miscommunications happened most frequently in Thailand, after being in the UK for seven years, I have realised how many words and phrases mean something different here than in Australia. It would seem that I'm doomed to be stuck in permanent cringe mode. But the large servings of humble pie have fuelled my hunger to listen more closely until I can finally understand how not to talk with a mouthful of foot.

Chapter 6 – The State of Affairs

Springvale, 1998

Amy and I head home in the car. An embarrassing amount of pink, plastic, noisy toys are piled around her, lovingly lavished by our asylum seeker and refugee friends. She is in heaven and looks angelic in her white taffeta ball gown and purple dungarees. Although it's way over the top, it's been a great day celebrating her second birthday at a city farm with many families from our neighbourhood. I'm looking in the rear-view mirror watching her clap along to kiddy-pop. I can't help but smile knowing our girl is surrounded by so much love.

In the 1990's and early 2000's the streets of Springvale were flooded with China White heroin. We found ourselves in a hotspot trying to support both people in the throws of heroin addiction and those wanting to detox and rehabilitate. Simultaneously asylum seekers and refugees were arriving from new places such as Burma, The Congo and East Timor. We were crossing over some really strange lines. Concurrently advocating for refugees and asylum seekers – trying to make them feel welcome, while supporting the most marginalised and broken Australians that often wreaked havoc on the neighbourhood in desperation to feed their drug habit. Some nights it really felt like we were living through an episode of *Twilight Zone*. On the day of the September 11 attacks I remember being awoken by Mary – who was going through her detox in our lounge room – saying planes had flown into the Twin towers. I assumed she was hallucinating and got up to prepare her morning medication just in time to see the second tower being hit. (Sadly this detox was not successful and after a few more wild years Mary died of a drug overdose leaving behind three grieving children).

In November 1991, a terrible tragedy known as the Dili massacre took place on the island of East Timor. Under Indonesian rule, soldiers opened fire on pro-independence protesters who had gathered in a cemetery, killing 250 of them. This, along with many other atrocities, was caught on film by an Australian journalist leading to thousands of East Timorese people fleeing to Australia. Six years later the refugees were still in limbo as the Australian Government tried to make a trade deal (believed to be about gas) in the Timor sea. Because of the politics of profit, these people, who should have clearly been given refugee status upon arrival, were threatened with deportation. Sadly, so much of what drives so-called humanitarian government policies in many developed countries is actually influenced by politics and nothing to do with compassion. This leaves thousands, maybe millions of refugees and asylum seekers in torturous insecurity around the world to this day.

Many of the survivors who fled East Timor to Australia seeking asylum were housed in temporary accommodation near our place in Springvale. Ash, and some of our team, did their best to advocate for their right to resettle permanently. But this turned into a decade-long battle with the heartless immigration department and money-driven politicians doing shady deals behind the scenes. Our East Timorese neighbours welcomed us and the team into the folds of their community, cooed over our baby daughter, and gave generous gifts despite being far from rich. They taught me that it really does take a village to raise a child. Their cultural expectations of shared living and shared responsibility to look out for each other's children left a lasting impression on me. It was incredible to think that while these amazing people were living with such uncertainty, faced with the horrors of what was happening to their loved ones back in East Timor, they continued to show such grace and care towards us. It put my minor daily anxieties to shame.

After years of battling, including a campaign thousands of Australians signed to say they would risk going to jail hiding the refugees rather than let them be sent back to East Timor, all of these families finally received their rights to stay and live in Australia. Years later, two of the now-adult children gave $400 to support Ash and I as we embarked on our journey to the UK. They wanted to give back now that they had finished their education and were in good jobs. They told us: "You helped us when we needed you. It's our turn to help you now."

It's easy to cast judgement on the Government, but the uncomfortable truth is that we are all guilty of being heartless at times. So many times I could have helped someone out and yet I chose to do something selfish instead. I've said I have no money to give to a worthwhile cause and gone straight to the shops and bought things I really didn't need. One of my most shameful moments – that I deeply regret to this day – was when I was driving home at night in the pouring rain with my Amy crying in the backseat. I couldn't wait to get home and put us both to bed after a shattering day when I saw him there, lying face-down, on the side of the road. The scene had obvious parallels to one of the most famous and best-loved bible stories of The Good Samaritan. But on that particular night I was running on empty and had little love left to give. I hate to admit that I drove past Dean and rushed home, and I slept straight through the night.

When next our paths crossed, I was overwhelmed with regret, waffling a long apology: "I'm so sorry I didn't do anything to help when I saw you there in the rain, mate. I had my daughter in the car. I was in a rush. It was late. I was so tired and, and, and …" Until he cut me off abruptly and said, "Don't feel sorry for me, I was high as a kite. I was lying there off my face having the time of my life. Feel sorry for me now, I need another hit and I'm starting to get really sick." Dean was a long-term heroin user.

In the weeks that followed there would be hundreds of overdoses in Springvale as the purity of pure China White heroin awash on the streets was too high. This batch was too strong even for the most hardened users. It was about this time when our little girl had to see her first dead body. Carrying her from the car to our flat, a neighbour who had no English motioned me over. Drug users were prolific up and down our street as they came to mix the heroin with water from the taps in the blocks of flats. Under the stairs was a guy who had overdosed. The stairs provided semi-privacy for people shooting up. Those who had collapsed veins from years of use resorted to more extreme places such as the veins on the tops of their feet or the large vein in the penis, some even rubbed the drug straight into their eyes! The syringe still stuck into his penis when we saw him and he was sprawled out in a broken, horrific way.

Dean helped me understand that whilst under the influence of heroin nothing else matters. He said we shouldn't be telling kids that drugs are bad but that drugs make you feel wonderful – too good – and that is why you shouldn't start taking them. It's impossible to give up that good feeling no matter how badly it messes up your life. My assumptions about what he needed and how I should help him were way off. Hearing his lived experiences turned my perceptions upside down. Working in a community blighted by drug use, I was constantly challenged by the desire to protect myself, my daughter and foster granddaughter from the chaos that drug users bring into your life. There is always a tension between what it takes to see justice and compassion outworked – and the desire to stay safe and protect your own.

Chapter 7 – Love Thy Neighbour

Springvale, 1994

A newly qualified social worker, I'm trying to prove my competence to colleagues in the courtroom. I look the part in my black suit. Out of the blue little Nina runs up and climbs all over me. She smells of strong chemical shampoo and loudly announces I must have missed some eggs when I de-loused her the night before because her hair's still itchy. I put my hand over her mouth and pray my boss didn't hear.

During my training as a social worker I sat through many lectures and workshops on the importance of maintaining professional boundaries. It made sense to me that we needed to protect both ourselves and the clients from co-dependence and unhealthy, unrealistic relationships. However, while living in Springvale we saw need around us that these lectures just did not address. For some families a small intervention made a huge difference. For instance, looking after someone's children for a week while they recovered from illness or driving kids to childcare while mum struggled with debilitating depression. Back then, and still to this day, the services which would really help people often didn't exist or had ridiculous waiting lists. Something as simple as lending a hand and being neighbourly had become frowned upon and fraught with judgement and fear.

When we were asked by Children's Services to take in a pregnant mum called Vera and her four children for a few weeks we were excited, even honoured, that they trusted us and that she would want to come and stay with us. Vera was at the last stage of her child protection intervention and if she coped well when the baby was born she was going to be allowed to keep her children. There were so many complex issues at play in this family but due to our young arrogance we felt we could do a good job at loving them. We believed love had the power to fix everything, and still do, but naively underestimated how hard the journey actually is …

The children's behaviour was extremely difficult. Their mum was also living in the house with us, so it was tough to know who was in charge and whether we should try and manage their behaviour. At times, I can be quite a 'potty mouth,' but the language that came from the four and five-year-old kids was enough to make your hair curl. We also had to think about how the behaviour impacted on the other kids we were caring for. Some days things were just completely out of control. Bedtime could not come around quickly enough. To make matters worse, Vera and all the children had scabies and head lice and many hours were spent trying to deal with the joy of this shared experience. (I bet you are feeling itchy now too!)

Vera had previously shared a house with a well-known meth and speed addict who was also an MMA fighter. He had been violent towards both her and the children. As a parting gift, when she eventually left, she had taken all his gym equipment and thrown it out. One day while I was (thankfully) at work, he tracked the family down to our Springvale address. He banged on the front door with a large tyre iron in his hand, threatening to kill the b**** for stealing his stuff. Ash was now a fully trained minister with a Master's Degree in Theology. But "Defending Yourself from a Drugged Up and Angry MMA Fighter" was not one of the subjects he had studied! He somehow blagged his way into calming this guy down, while the mum and her two smallest children cowered in tears in our outdoor toilet. Eventually, and as if by some miracle, this guy started ranting, "Call the police! Call the police! I want her charged with robbery" which was something Ash was extremely happy to do. By the time the police came to take him away, Ash had calmed him down even further by giving him a cup of tea (again a tactic not often taught at seminary but one that should definitely be added to the curriculum). Coming home from work to hear both Ash and Vera's version of events I did wonder if some of our professional boundaries might need to be looked at again!

Later that month, I came home to find her ironing the crotch of her knickers on my lovely new ironing board. She looked up at me with a smile and said, "Glad you're back to watch the kids. My waters have just broken and soaked my pants so I'm just drying them then I need to go and have this baby." I nearly gagged at the thought of her amniotic fluids all over my nice couch and happily sent her off to the hospital before binning the ironing board.

As I look back on my life there's a common theme of feeling torn between being a compassionate neighbour and a professional caseworker. I realise now that a lot of the assumptions I made about the clients I worked with back then; were unfairly judgemental. Especially as I had no parenting experience myself at that point (although we had fostered many babies and teenagers). The bible tells us: "Judge not lest you be judged". So much of my life has been about judging others and, in some way, writing this book is a kind of penance as I put my life and failings out there to be judged publicly too.

In the 90s, the trend was to professionalise 'help' in community development and youth work. People who were the natural helpers of neighbourhoods – the community glue – went into professional training; driven by compassion and the desire to make a difference. At the same time, Australia saw an increase in government funding to churches to help run welfare provisions. The result was services run by churches became more privatised and professional. Voluntary, friendship-style help became less available.

In the UK this was further exacerbated by a highly risk-averse culture. "Thou shalt not take any risks!" feels like the 11th commandment: This is the very opposite of the life of Jesus, whom we in the church profess to follow! I'm not advocating being irresponsible and intentionally dangerous. Obvious dangers need to be mitigated. But to think we can truly love and support others without taking any risks at all – that would make us naive.

When my Dad became unemployed in his 50s he noticed a neighbour struggling to cut their grass with an old mower. He offered to fix the lawn mower to keep himself busy. He quickly realised the man had special learning needs and his partner was blind with other additional needs. They had a small child and generally struggled with life. He befriended them and invited them over for meals. This family did have a number of support workers and social workers involved with them. However, their crisis times when they needed help did not usually happen on weekdays between 9-5pm but at night or on weekends. With no relatives nearby to help, my Mum and Dad became family to them. They were often called over late at night to help support with one issue or another. When their relationship broke down the blind mother was left trying to raise the active young boy on her own. As the child grew, my parents asked people from their church to help with driving him and his mum to children's programmes and Sunday school. The community was encouraged to gather around this mother and her son, and many professional boundaries were crossed.

As a result of this strong bond, when the difficult teenage years hit, this young man had stable people around him to help get him out of trouble or drive him to his apprenticeship when he wouldn't get out of bed on time. My Mum's proudest moment was to see him complete his apprenticeship and make a life for himself. This young man who, would have been destined for foster care and (if our experience is anything to go by) quite probably have ended up in prison, is now a qualified mechanic, married to a lovely young woman and doing well enough to help his mum out. Although there is *most definitely* a role for professional social workers (of which I am one!) there is a gap between what families really need to thrive and what services responsible for child safety are actually able to do. I think community is the key to this. Neighbours that can form a circle of support around the most vulnerable in the community to offer help when crisis times hit. Professional services can help. They can link those needs to support; but their role is limited by their work remit and employed hours. There are a number of amazing programmes that now recognise the need to respond to the gaps that the over-professionalising of help has created. **Coach** (Australia) https://www.coachnetwork.org/about-us/ and **Safe Families for Children** (UK) https://safe-families.org are two great organisations. But I must confess to me it is sad that we need programmes to remind us to love our neighbour!

Chapter 8 – Down the Drain

Klong Toey, 2011

It's the middle of the night. I am laying wide awake in our little home, the size of four double beds. Through the thin walls I can hear the excruciating noises of a woman being badly beaten by her partner. It's pitch black and the little window we have is painted shut. Staring through the darkness I'm wondering how exposure to these sounds is going to affect my kids.

Raising my kids in the heart of a slum was not easy. Nor an easy decision. But, at least, in the absence of social services, the art of neighbourliness is not forgotten in Klong Toey. When my son Aiden was 18 months old, I experienced warm-hearted community support first hand after having a complete public meltdown.

A kind neighbour had fixed up and given Aiden a brightly coloured plastic tricycle. And he loved nothing more than to toddle around pushing it through the narrow pathways in the slum. These lanes are made up of concrete blocks, wooden planks, lots of rubbish, dirty water and cat pee. That particular morning, I was standing chatting to some friends watching Aiden play when, quick as a flash, he tripped over his plastic bike and landed head-first into an open sewer. Most of the open sewers had been covered up after the big floods in 2002. But at the front of each house was a small section left open for dishwashing and laundry water. We all washed our dishes in big plastic tubs. I had managed to score a vintage twin tub washing machine that had to be filled by hand; but at least spun empty through a drain hose into the open drain.

I screamed in horror.

At least a dozen neighbours came running to pull him out. The overwhelming crowd of helpers caused big scratches on his back as he was inadvertently dragged across rough edges of wood covering the rest of the sewer. I ran with him into the house and washed the big black chunks of filth from his face and teeth. Wiping his wounds clean with alcohol wipes while a crowd of onlookers all tried to stop him from screaming yet making him scream more. Some old ladies thought pinching his cheeks and growling at him would do the trick!

Aiden, unlike me, bounced back. The next day he was back outside fearlessly pushing his plastic bike around the exact same area. I stood over the open sewer to ensure he couldn't fall in. One of the neighbours pointed to where I was standing. A large, bloated rat's body floated in the black water. She laughed and said: "Look what that *farang* [foreigner] did. He killed a rat!" I prayed that whatever diseases were emanating from the carcass had not gone up my son's nose or into his mouth. I would like to say I had faith, but the truth is I stayed awake most of the next few nights checking Aiden's temperature to make sure he was not dying.

There were quite a few moments like this during our time in the slum. They make me shudder to recall. But every time my amazing neighbours were there to help get me or my kids to hospital. The kids only ever seemed to need stitches when Ash was away travelling! But there was always a bevy of willing motorbike drivers there for me at these times. And there was always a gang of well-meaning women to tell me off after we returned from the hospital. I was learning that I had to let our neighbours help and care for our family even if that meant getting lectured sometimes. Mutually beneficial equal relationships are far healthier than having fixed givers and receivers.

Living in our second house in Klong Toey also put us on a fast track to letting go of the rest of our Western concept of privacy. We literally lived in an open house. The front wall consisted of an open-up gate so everyone could see and hear everything we did. We only closed it at night. It would have been unbearably hot to close it in the day – and night was not much better! The proximity of people, and the way the slum houses are all jumbled together, meant we would often see the best and the worst events of our neighbour's lives unfold within the space of a single day. Tragedies and miracles overlapped. We often felt robbed of ever having the chance to truly celebrate as the surrounding suffering would simultaneously be so sobering. I came to wonder if us humans are only capable of experiencing true joy once we have known deep pain. That thought doesn't make the agony of injustice and suffering any easier to bear. But it comforts me that God is not absent in the midst of it. This balancing contrast gave us even more reason to lean into the discomfort and do what we could, rather that avoid being there altogether. I have learnt that I am far more resilient than I ever thought. I'm not special in that way at all. We all have it in us. Most people in wealthy developed countries have just never get to realise how hardy they can be. Society shields us from the uncomfortable. If I'm honest, the most difficult thing I have ever done is not move into a slum in Asia (as that was fun and exciting most of the time) but it was actually packing up my whole slum life and moving to the UK to start over at 45 years old.

Chapter 9 – Black Dog vs Pug

Winson Green, 2015

Hiding in my dark bedroom, bingeing boxsets, trying to escape my new reality. I can feel judgement even from Netflix as it keeps flashing the incredulous message: "Are you still watching?!" I am homesick for Thailand. I am missing my daughter who is thousands of miles away in Australia. I'm struggling to try and like my job, and England's grey days are starting to chew at my soul.

When we first arrived in Birmingham, the grief of saying goodbye to Thailand hounded me. I was putting in my best efforts to 'fake it till I make it' with the feelings of homesickness while trying to adjust and survive. But as life became slowly more 'normal' it began to get the better of me. The long dark months of adjustment to life in the West after more than 12 years in tropical Asia. To living through winter where the cold light only manages to hold on for a few short hours. It became the hardest thing I've ever done in my life. Six-months had passed since we left Klong Toey and the organisation we founded and ran for 22 years; the delayed grief was just starting to set in.

From the depths of my own despair I still marvelled at Aiden's adjustment. At 10 years old he had left the only home he had ever known. His first language is Thai but he spoke good English and fortunately is a generally happy kid. So the toughest times were when homesickness hit him too. I struggled to comfort him as my own sadness was overwhelming. When he found out we were leaving Thailand, Aiden had channelled all of his sadness into not wanting to leave behind his slum-dog, Candy. So our saving grace in the UK was buying a little pug called Yoda.

My family had nagged me for years to get a dog in Klong Toey. But I'm not really an animal lover, and honestly, I felt so overwhelmed by the unmet needs of people that I could not see a reason to add pets into the mix! Even so, it would appear I'm not as hard-arsed as I thought because, when Amy turned 10, I finally gave in and let her buy a dog. Many months of research led up to the momentous day. Amy settled on a Pomeranian. We went to Chatuchak, the large weekend market that sells everything you can imagine (including smuggled rare Australian wildlife). And there she was. The exact dog Amy had her eye on. 'She's a three-month-old Pomeranian', the young man said with a sweet smile. She was wearing a little pink dress, with pink bows in her fluffy fur. Amy happily spent the rest of her pocket money buying cute little dog accessories, including, but not limited to: A Tutu, a dog Bikini and a pink diamante-encrusted lead with matching collar. A few days later we took Candy to a local vet to get some worming pills and necessary shots. Well – we certainly got more than we bargained for. It turns out that Candy was only about one-month-old – hence the fluffy fur. The vet carefully peeled off some tape hidden in her long fur on her head, huge ears flopped down! It was instantly obvious that she was a mix of Thai street dog and a fur ball. It also turned out that Candy was a male! Amy decided it was culturally appropriate to keep the name and the pink outfits and Candy became our *katoey* ladyboy dog. Ash, who was the only one who ever walked her, was never overly impressed with her pink outfits that made it look like he was walking a pampered cat.

As much as we loved Candy, she was already eight years old when we moved from Thailand and was struggling with health issues. The move to the UK would have finished her off. So, we gave her to the guy tasked with setting up IKEA in Thailand. She got to live out her days in luxury within view of my favourite shop.

So Yoda the Pug was, for Aiden, the fulfilment of a promise we made to help with the transition. Like most things, I hadn't thought it through, and I nearly had a fit when I realised he would cost more than our car! But, I think much of his distress about leaving the dog was also masking something he couldn't quite articulate. We had two foster sons a year younger than Aiden, one who had been with us for three years and the other for almost two years. Since his sister left to live in Australia when she was 16, these boys were family to Aiden. It was heart-breaking for all concerned and especially as one of the little boys went to live with his Grandmother in less than ideal circumstances. This was a really difficult situation. I have many regrets and have shed many tears over the whole process. However, my priority was Aiden. He had been ripped from everything he knew in life and moved across the world to a country he had no connection with.

Our grotty new accommodation in the UK didn't make things any easier. While I initially liked the house and thought a few things just needed fixing. It soon became apparent that there were serious issues such as leaking gas and electrical faults that made living there quite dangerous. I was also in for the harsh realisation that, while laws exist that are supposed to protect tenants, there is no one to enforce them in Birmingham. Landlords can literally do whatever they like without fear of punishment. I tried to work up some enthusiasm about buying new flat-pack furniture to disguise the terrible state of the rental property. Although it is a magical place to me, IKEA can't perform miracles. There was a big hole kicked out of our bedroom door, a weird smell in the front room and every plug socket was blackened from previous electrical fires. The house was overrun with mice and rats, just like our slum home. After four months it became too dangerous to turn the heating on as it turned out the weird smell was a gas leak and every time British Gas came and capped the supply the landlord would just come back and uncap it. He eventually threatened to kick us out if we called them again.

We were starting from scratch and didn't have spare money to just up and move out. So we went without gas for the last few months until we could get another place. However, in all these trials I felt God was with us. We had a taste of what so many migrants and refugees face when they arrive in our community. Like them, we were so grateful to even get a house as we had no rental references or credit history. We had to pay six months' rent in advance which meant we would get nothing back if we moved. So many newly arrived migrants in our community put up with terrible landlords and horrendous conditions for the same reasons. Unlike many of them, we were really lucky to be part of a church network. Through that we met one of the greatest gifts God has given us and our community: John Harrison. John is 'Mr Fix It' and he came to our rescue many times to get our power working, fix broken doors and do plumbing. The only benefit of having a truly dilapidated house was that, over the many times John was called to our house, we became great friends. John is now a key member of the team at Newbigin House and most definitely part of our family.

When we arrived in Birmingham, I hoped, assumed even, that the hard-won lessons from Springvale and Klong Toey would be transferable and that I would have something of worth to contribute. But first I had to get over the rude awakening of becoming an employee of someone else's organisation. Through some connections, I was offered a role as a chaplain/hub leader for a school in Winson Green. It is true to say that my hyperactive personality was definitely the wrong fit for working within the structures of a large national charity in a British primary school. The long-suffering head teacher was gracious and my line-manager handled me as best they could, but the three years I worked there was one giant learning curve for everyone.

I realised very quickly, and with great shock, that much of the same poverty we had seen in Thailand was evident in this part of Birmingham. England had suffered a decade of austerity that had been particularly cruel to the poorest members of society. The systems that I had expected to be there to protect children and families were incredibly broken. I soon discovered that this next chapter of my life was going to be the most challenging and intense ever. With the added dimension of, yet again, being a fish out of water. In working-class Springvale, people generally say exactly what they think. Australians generally have a more egalitarian approach to giving opinions. Arriving in the UK I realised, often too late, that if you spoke your mind or offered unsolicited advice around key decisions, people would generally be taken aback. They might not say anything to your face, but you'd be branded 'brash'.

The weeks passed and I began to see the underbelly of life in Birmingham. I was not so much disturbed by the poverty as I was by the systemic acceptance that "this is just how life is". Many soul-destroying conversations with others in the welfare and charity sector revealed a defeated credence that the majority of the funding goes to pay middle class professional helpers' salaries. That the resources rarely trickle down to actually meet the urgent needs of those who are thrown on the trash heap of society. I have sadly learnt not to be surprised by the church's complicity in all this. Birmingham – always full of surprises – is however filled with some amazing Godly people quietly working away to fight for change and model new ways forward. But the task is huge. This discovery of like-minded missionaries started to stir something in me and eventually became a driving factor in me finding a way back to my calling and life's purpose.

I believe that so many of us never discover the true capacity we have and therefore miss out on so much of what life has to offer. Highly risk-averse cultural contexts throughout the developed world often prevent us from experiencing the necessary suffering that is required for us to see how truly compassionate, resourceful and determined we can be. I've met amazingly strong people over the years and the common thread in all of them is that they have been through some incredible sadness and suffering.

The terrible things I have been exposed to here in the UK, and the brutality and poverty I saw in Thailand have made me realise more than ever that: "Where we stand determines what we see". What a privilege I have had to be living alongside those who have been overlooked. Having my eyes opened to the harsh reality of life for most of the people in the world.

Although I was tired and a bit bruised and battered, I knew in my heart that this is what God had made me for. I had an idea that Winson Green was exactly where I should be. Pomeranians and Pugs can't cure the black dog of depression but reawakening to a sense of spiritual purpose – that can really help.

Chapter 10 – A Lesson in Living and Dying

Klong Toey, 2012

The sweat is pouring off my face. I'm trying not to vomit at the smell of the poo smeared all over his body. Managing to get the nappy off during the night he had smeared his plentiful faeces all over himself. I'm cutting the poo coloured bandages off his large diabetic ulcers and he is giggling like a small child. Happy for human touch and knowing some food is waiting for him at the end of all this. As I free the last bandage and turn the shower on to wash it all away I make the mistake of wiping sweat from my eyes forgetting my gloves are covered in poo and pus.

Pi Bu was our neighbour for several years. His sister was a good friend of mine and they lived opposite us. He was a hard-drinking, fast-living, grumpy motorbike taxi driver who we only really interacted with to say hello. Sometimes he would yell at the kids who would congregate in front of our house when they leaned up against his parked motorbike. To be honest I was pretty scared of him. The hard-living and whisky drinking had left him with severe pancreatitis and diabetes. When we were away in Australia, he fell into a diabetic coma from unmanaged sugar levels and was taken to hospital. They revived him but not before he suffered significant brain damage that left him with complete loss of impulse control and a childlike level of cognitive functioning. He was sent home for his sister, Pi Sim to look after. Pi Sim is one of the strongest, bravest and, at times, the scariest women I know. Due to lack of welfare support in Thailand she was already caring for her adult daughter, her granddaughter, both of Pi Bu's sons (who were regularly in and out of jail) *and* a new baby when her son also went to prison and his very young girlfriend couldn't cope. She had just nursed their mother through an end of life illness without any financial or practical help from Pi Bu. Now she was left to care for a man who ate constantly then wandered off and smeared his faeces all over the place. Unsurprisingly this led to conflicts with the neighbours who were utterly repulsed by him. She was left with no option but to lock him in a small room in their tin-shack slum house.

It is common in Klong Toey for grandparents to be left with their grandchildren. Particularly when relationships break up. The prevalence of polygamy further exacerbates this as women become a *mia noi* (minor wife) or a *gik* (girlfriend on the side). Often the men don't want the responsibility of the children from the previous relationship. There are always some exceptions to this. We know a few amazing guys who have taken on their new partner's children in Thailand. However, for every one of these guys we know at least 10 elderly people who have been dumped with the care and responsibility of not just one, but numerous grandchildren, nephews and nieces. Often the parents have been imprisoned, died or simply disappeared to start a new life.

Every morning at 4.30am Pi Sim was up and off to the market to support her family by selling breakfast porridge rice called *jok*. By 5.30am she would have a delicious pot of boiling congee rice ready to sell to everyone heading off to school and work. Her little shop, right opposite her house, provided a good living (fortunately!). It was the place where neighbours congregated each day. I learnt so much about the community – all the drama going on – just sitting on my doorstep with my morning coffee listening to the gossip. It was an amazing way to make connections with people in need of support. Pi Sim was always making introductions to help me help those neighbours most in need. In the evening I would sit outside, completely exhausted after the drama and heat that each day brought, as she sold BBQ chicken wings. I hadn't seen Pi Bu for a few weeks and Pi Sim said he was too ill now to walk around. But that evening she teared up and told me just how hard it had been trying to manage him. Customers were boycotting her shop because the smell of faeces was unbearable, and he could be heard banging on the tin wall to be let out which was making people feel uncomfortable. I asked if she would like me to help, and she said actually yes. In Thai culture it is considered a sin to interfere with other people's family business; and this was always a delicate thing to negotiate. I was becoming increasingly aware that we never really understood what the implications of our actions were.

The next morning my friend Lyn came to visit to check up on a child she was helping support after an operation. She was part of a group of women I dubbed 'The Fabulous Four'. (Lyn, Cheryl, Kirsten and Nicole). They were the best volunteers you could ever hope for. Four expats or 'trailing spouses' as their husband's work had brought them here. They were incredibly passionate and gifted in a variety of areas, and somehow I was lucky enough to have them around us as friends and volunteers! Lyn was a Physiotherapist from the UK helping me with kids, and some adults, who needed operations for such things as broken bones, hip dysplasia and TB in the bone (just to mention a few things). There are some very lucky young adults today in Klong Toey able to walk (and work) thanks to her!

Anyway! Lyn and I could hear Pi Bu groaning and crying from inside Pi Sim's house. I suggested we go in and check on him. Pi Sim unlocked the room. The smell assaulted us before our eyes adjusted to the half light. We then saw what looked like a scene from a horror movie. A skeletal man was lying on the floor in a pool of urine. He had on a partially torn adult diaper. His face was covered in poo. We decided we should take him to hospital, so I looked around for something to transport him on. Opposite the house I found an old food trolley. We laid an old cane mat down in an attempt to make it a bit more comfortable. As the two of us lifted him up to move him, the heavily soaked and torn diaper fell off, splashing the urine from the ground into my face. Pi Bu cried out in pain as my fingers sunk about an inch deep into large leg ulcers that I had not noticed at the back of his legs.

We proceeded to delicately move him from the trolley to Lyn's (lovely) car. I remember thinking how amazing she was that she didn't seem to mind at all about the poo and wee and pus going everywhere. She kept saying: "Please don't die on us. Please don't die." Somehow in a blur we managed to get through the Bangkok traffic to a private Catholic hospital nearby. It wasn't as expensive as the posh one we usually went to, but we knew we were going to have to pay for this hospitalisation and treatment, which could run into thousands of dollars even in Bangkok. We knew that he would just be left to die in pain if we took him to the free Government hospital. So, with no family members able to help financially, this was on us.

Pi Bu was cleaned up and given the required medical treatment. Once his diabetes was under control, he started to improve. Now we were faced with a bigger dilemma. After two weeks in hospital and a $2000 bill, he needed to be discharged. But we didn't want the burden of his care to fall on his sister, Pi Sim. It was agreed that I would take Pi Bu into our house each morning to wash and clean him while Pi Sim cooked and sold food. I would shower him, re-bandage the stubborn diabetic ulcers and give him his injections. Then he could sit, all clean and smelling like roses, to have breakfast with Ash while I disposed of the poo covered clothes and bandages. After finishing selling her food Pi Sim would totally wash out his room, dispose of the latest poo covered bedding, reset the room and lock him back in while I went off to work. Many days I would receive a call to say he had climbed out the window or made a hole in the wall and was now covered in poo sitting at someone's house or shop refusing to leave. Sadly, on some of these occasions he was beaten by neighbours trying to get him and his smell away from their house. Mentally, he was like a stubborn three-year-old and didn't understand. Each evening we would repeat the same poo-covered story – trying all kinds of tactics to keep the nappy on – such as gaffer tape and even superglue. But he always managed to get it off and wipe shit everywhere!

In my mind I had been doing this for what felt like years. In fact, it was only a few months and then we were off to Australia for a fundraising trip. I felt so bad leaving the burden with Pi Sim and tried in vain to pay someone to help her. But this would never work for many deeply-held cultural reasons due to shame and Karmic beliefs.

After returning from Australia it was clear that Pi Bu was in a terrible state again, and I knew that another hospital trip –

while probably making him temporarily well again – would prolong the suffering. To this day I live with the guilt that I chose to let him die. I had always thought of myself as pro-life but what kind of life was this? Not just for him but for the 12 people most affected by his needs? What right did I have to extend the burden for this family? By now Pi Sim had another mouth to feed as another grandchild had been born and another on the way, so the pressure was unbearable.

Within a few days of our return, Pi Bu became unconscious and passed away. I heard the cries and sobs at about 5am and went into the house. A strange mix of sadness, guilt and relief washed over me. I had really come to love this guy through all the weird awkward poo and pus moments. There had been glimpses of a sweet man deep inside there. Had his circumstance of birth been different it may have emerged. Instead, crime, drugs and alcohol peppered his life and created a harsh personality like so many men born into slum life. The funeral was a celebration after a few awkward moments. Too much formaldehyde had been injected into his emaciated body. As we sat by his open casket at the temple one of the kids started screaming that a ghost was coming out of his mouth. I looked and realised the excess formaldehyde was gurgling out of his very firm mouth. I tried to stop this by using an incense stick to push a bit of tissue into his mouth. I'm not sure how many taboos I was breaking, but it seemed to calm everyone down.

Pi Sim and I were already close. She was one of only a very few Thai neighbours who would yell at me, tell me off and put me straight when I did something wrong – which was often. Going through the struggle with Pi Bu together cemented our friendship that remains strong to this day.

I learnt two important things from this that have helped me in my work in the UK. Never judge what you see without knowing the whole story. Pi Sim was not cruel and hateful but rather a fighter who used all her energy to care for her kids and grandkids; working day and night just to feed everyone. She is a hero – someone who could have just given up on life. If I had her life, I probably would have. But instead she fights on.

As I write this, she is at home sweating through the Thai hot season in her tiny tin shack trying to deal with what the Thai Government lockdown during the Coronavirus pandemic and what that will do to her already meagre income.

I also learnt that I am actually pro-choice. This can seem controversial as a Christian and may be unwise to confess. But I believe that God intends people to have truly abundant life. What right do I have to decide that for others? To make that a burden for others? What I would and could do as a person with resources cannot be imposed on those who have none of the same options I have. Perhaps we cannot truly be pro-life unless we are personally willing to take in the unwanted babies and elderly chronically ill folk and care for them ourselves?

With my mum and brother and sister (1973) – my brother Brendan would join us 14 years later to complete the family.

Ready for my first day of school: Mornington, Australia (1974)

As a family we spent some time in Holland when I was 7 (I'm on the right).

Married December 2nd 1989

With Metus and some of our other foster kids (1993)

Amy celebrating her first birthday in Vietnam (1997)

Ash's graduation with Lisa, Belinda, Brooke, Beau and Bonnie, Denise and Christine and my dad and Ash's dad (1995)

Metus and Denise at Christine's christening (1995)

Amy with patients at the AIDS hospice (1999)

My twin tub washing machine – even though I had to fill it with a bucket it made life a bit easier (2002)

Aiden 2 weeks old (2003)

Amy and Aiden on their way to school with Pi Kare (2005)

Aiden with Poo's children Best and Boss who are like family to us (2005)

Aiden and Best (2007)

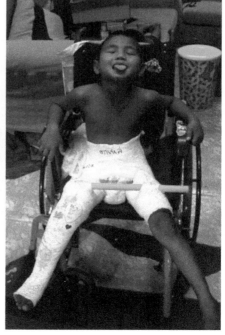

Little Orr with his spica plaster cast being his cheeky self (2010)

The Bangkok launch of "Cooking with Poo" with Poo, Blah and Noi – organised by the amazing Louisa Warr and Aela Streiff (2011)

Cheryl Stansfield who continues to support the families in the Klong Toey Slum, and the brilliant Debbie Oakes, my editor.

Pi Sim and the amazing Liz Maher

Aiden with our dog Candy and his foster brothers. Bangkok (2012)

Poo and Kare and the boys saying goodbye to Aiden and I as we left Thailand, broke our hearts (2014)

Returning to Bangkok after 3 years. With Kook and Tai (2017)

Christians at Pride – with Lizzie and Naomi, my good friend Matt, and Trey Hall an amazing Methodist Minister (2018)

With Brooke and her three kids and Bonnie – as well as Belinda's sister and mother 2018. (Just missing Beau from this picture.)

With Amy and Rob the day they got engaged (2019)

With Sally Man and Jessica Craig in Greece as they helped ply this book from me (2019)

Making my son-in law walk alpacas in the rain after a 36 hour journey from Australia – welcome to England and to our crazy family.

Alpacas guarding the front door in Birmingham (2021)

Chapter 11 – Friends and Neighbours

Winson Green, 2013

Watching through the school fence I see my precious little boy facing off with a much larger kid. I gasp to see the anger on Aiden's face as they start to push and shove each other. Thankfully a teacher steps in. It's only a year since the academy chain I work for took over this rough school. Since then things have improved a lot – but there's still work to do. Suddenly, my guilt at bringing Aiden here, watching him struggle with the new system and then the toughness of the older kids, is overwhelming.

January is the coldest month of the year and we are three winter months into our new life in the UK. Aiden has hit a real low and is refusing to go to school. Being dyspraxic and dyslexic the rote learning, exam-based style of the British school system is crushing him. We realise, to get the support he desperately needs, he has to change schools. Finding the right school is one thing – struggling with what it means to raise the required school fees – quite another. Although we have both started earning decent incomes; there is nothing in our bank account and Amy also needs financial support while studying at university in Australia. Beginning again from scratch at 45 years old is proving much harder than we anticipated.

With nothing to lose but hope, we met with the head teacher. He asks about our work in Thailand and what we are doing in the UK. He carefully listens as we explain our predicament before he sends us out of the room to interview Aiden. Our intention was to ask to pay the fees in instalments. But what he says when he calls us back in the room, knocks our socks off. "I don't believe in God – but just in case he's real – I'd better be helping you out. Aiden can start in year six on Monday, and we won't charge you. Once he attends high school we will charge you £1000 a term [a fraction of the actual fees!]." Ash promptly burst into tears. At that moment I realised just how much pressure he felt to make it OK for Aiden and I to be in the UK. I hadn't given his feelings of responsibility a second thought. I was focused so much on our homesickness for Thailand, how much we were missing our friends and feeling like we had been ripped out of our lives without any choice. This was the moment that my anger about all that started to chip away. It was, and is, little moments like this that God shows up. I had been trying to pretend, even to myself, I was not deeply resentful at leaving all I know and love in Thailand, but Ash had felt it.

During the next difficult 12 months of adjustment, God turned up in this way many times. It always reminds me that I can run but I cannot hide.

Just as my resentment started to thaw and I began to find my place in Birmingham; Ash's world imploded. The situation at the college he had so enthusiastically come to work for changed fast. It rapidly became apparent that it was not the place where he could use his gifts and skills as he had imagined. By the end of 2015 have found ourselves in dire straits with loads of debt, a new mortgage (that we were blessed to get at this late stage in life) and on a single income – mine. Unfortunately for me I had also somehow convinced myself that I would not have to work at the school for long. The prospect of being locked into doing it long-term was crushing. Amy was really struggling in Australia. Her anxiety was peaking and we suspect she was using drugs to self-medicate. I was so worried about her I was too scared to turn my phone off at night. I wanted to fly over and scoop her up in my arms but there was no money for the huge airfare, and I had to work. Some friends of ours generously chipped in, and we are able to send Ash over for a few weeks, which comforted me a little.

When he returned, it was time for him to look for work and deal with the train wreck that life had become in Birmingham. Fortunately, we felt God pulling strings behind the scenes because Ash was offered a full-time job as a 'Through The Gate Mentor' and Chaplain working at the prison just at the end of our road.

Our new home had three bedrooms and an extension into the back yard. After the shack we lived in in Klong Toey, and the terrible first house we rented around the corner, I felt like I was living the middle-class dream. In truth, next door, 13 men were sharing one house and would crash about loudly after late-night shifts, and we witness several drug raids on our street. But it was a good space in the right place, giving us a decent base to build upon. And, let's face it, I am always in my element in the middle of the crazy action.

A local mum, Ruth befriended us and would bring her kids over to play. John-mr fix it, was always around in the background doing practical jobs. Another new friend, Simone, popped in regularly and my boss Kat had also become a good friend and great support. I started a local youth club where teenagers from the neighbourhood could meet at our house every Saturday night and, along with the help of my teammate Sam, we would take them out to do fun activities. Finally, we were finding our way back to who we are. Finally, we were developing proper friendships. The first community meal in our new home sealed it. Although true to form, I manage to burn most of it, no one seemed to mind and the only problem was we now had too many new friends to fit into our house!

Later that year, after much hard lobbying and negotiating by Ash, we were offered the chance to rent a detached six-bedroom vicarage with a large garden just up the road. It's in the former parish of a famous British missionary, called Leslie Newbigin, so we got permission to rename it 'Newbigin House'.

April 2016. After only 10 months living in our own little home, we moved into Newbigin House. By the end of that year we had been joined by live-in teammates Gwen and John (and since then have added others). Gwen is an incredible to gift to our family and our community and she, thankfully, loves animals. Over the next year we managed to grow an urban farm of lambs, goats, alpacas, lizards, a hedgehog and some Madagascan hissing cockroaches to keep Yoda the Pug company. Despite living in a suburban zoo, I still don't really like animals! Nevertheless, the social enterprise part of the charity I worked for, 'Animal Encounters' really took off. Thankfully Gwen liked caring for them. Someone had to take the animals home from the school during the holidays and weekends, so they all become part-time house pets. Once, when I was away for two weeks, the team accepted a donation of two corn snakes and a python. Growing up in Australia you are taught *all snakes will kill you*. So getting over the fear of that message is hard work. Also, they needed to be fed mice and rats which I discover have also been 'kindly' donated and now filled my freezer. The next challenge was they needed to be defrosted and then dangled, as if alive, for the snakes to show any interest! I had a great idea – the microwave will do the trick! One exploding rat later and my friend Femmy and I run from the house and almost vomit. I know exactly what to do and, once again, my trusty hair dryer worked wonders. As you can probably guess, the snakes were soon donated to someone else!

Animal Encounters, started with a couple of permanent resident alpacas because I thought it would be a great way of meeting people in the neighbourhood. I remember driving to Essex with my friend Meg to pick up the first ones. I knew very little about what to do with an alpaca but had been watching loads of YouTube clips. Being Australian, people assume we know about farms and animals. Faking it until making it, is my super power and it gave me a bit of Dutch-courage. So now we have five alpacas, 3 living in our garden and are known locally as 'the crazy alpaca house'. Last week there was a major police incident in the neighbourhood. The alpacas can be seen in all the news reports staring at the police as they comb the street for forensic evidence.

During one of the many pandemic lockdowns we were awoken to discover intruders in our house. The police arrived in seconds, jumping our back fence to chase the intruders down. One officer fell backwards into the mud after coming face-to-face with a very friendly alpaca who was wondering what all the fuss was about. It certainly gave everyone a good laugh during what was a scary and tense situation. They have been a great way to create bonds, momentum and energy for our neighbourhood identity and activities. (Especially on the occasions when they escape the garden and the whole neighbourhood gets involved in bringing them back home!)

Each year, for the last five years, we have also taken in a number of orphaned or *cade* new-born lambs from my friend's farm. We get the neighbours and local schools to adopt, help bottle-feed, care for and walk them around. They actually become as tame as dogs and only look slightly ridiculous being walked around the inner city neighbourhood streets wearing adult diapers (health and safety!) When a 40 kg lamb tries to sit on your lap when you are watching TV it's a bit of a challenge though. The Animal Encounters social enterprise became so successful that we often had to say no to bookings and events. More and more groups wanted our travelling road show of weird and bizarre pets on leads. Our attempt to train chickens to walk on a lead has been the only thing that has almost ended in disaster. We didn't realise they would try to fly and almost strangle themselves. So we leave them to their eggs.

Newbigin House quickly filled with people as well as animals. As we have learnt before, everyone brings their own set of unique gifts and talents just waiting to be shaken into life. Ruth started an after-school kid's craft club, so we were all constantly covered in glitter. Our friend, Prince launched a personal training company to get himself back on his feet after getting out of prison. Devina started a pop-up hairdressing salon to keep her active and use her skills to make women feel wonderful. The women from the *Flavours of Winson Green* Cooking Enterprise, developed a catering arm, adding events to their already successful cooking school. Christopher tried his hand at making concrete furniture in order to keep off drugs and, a music group for mental health recovery is making songs in our garden. As I write this our new blacksmithing project can be heard banging hot metal into hangers and hooks in the garden. We've tried all the ideas our neighbours have come up with. For every five things we've attempted, maybe three things have failed. But that's good-going in my experience. Ash calls it a seedbed because we created fertile ground to feed local people's ideas with hope to grow. He recently launched a new charity by the same name (seedbeds. org) to share our learning and encourage other Christians to innovate community-building enterprises.

These enterprises also revealed the need to upskill people who can in turn help others to incubate their dreams. To this end, Ash developed an Urban Change Makers course (urbanchangemakers.org) This is a one-year development course that trains people to work in teams in their local neighbourhoods to dream up ways to launch innovative new enterprises.

At a certain point even the spacious Newbigin House became too full to fit everyone. So we ran a crowdfunding campaign to purchase a Mongolian Yurt (round tent). We put it in the front garden and started our Sunday gathering there. We invited people who "don't do church" to meet together in the yurt after a shared meal. It's called 'Church in A Yurt'. It's become a sacred and special place that has sparked some therapeutic groups such as a music group called Rock the Yurt, and a men's mental health support group. During the first wave of the Covid-19 crisis in March 2020 we were able to run our food parcel distribution from there too.

Newbigin House has become a safe place where we can test organic ways to transform our community, with no external pressure to succeed, or reach 'outcome targets'. It is a good 'bumping space'. Somewhere to meet all the diverse local characters. Our dream is for it to continue to be a welcoming hub at the heart of our community. A space where people can escape their cramped homes and lack of space. Our downstairs room is a home-from-home for anyone who needs a place to be. Most nights during summer you can find people from the neighbourhood in our back garden around the BBQ.

After being beaten down by those early years in Birmingham, I'm so grateful that we managed to stick it out long enough to see good fruit finally flourish. I have learnt that in order to stay on track, and avoid distractions, I must hold on to my 'why?' When the road gets rough, I remember the reason I started all this in the first place: The commitment to the promise I made as a teenager and inspiration from my Faith is what pushes me on. When I'm tempted to run away, I remember that my work is also a legacy of the tragic life and death of our beloved foster son Metus. Then, by God's Grace, I am compelled forward to try and make the world a better place for the all Metus' of the future.

Chapter 12 – Life Changing Loss

Springvale, 1994

Screams reach down the hall and pierce my ears with the gut-wrenching tenacity of nails scratching a blackboard. Desolation fills my heart as I watch the nurses roughly restrain him. The psych ward is grim and stinks of bleach. It is hard to see this as a place of recovery and I dread to think about what happens to most of the young people here when they are released.

Metuakore's grandparents moved to Australia from the Cook Islands with a total of 18 children and grandchildren. Metuakore ('Metus' was his nickname) was a bit lost in the crowd. When his grandfather asked us to look after him, we were honoured and excited. He was such a lovely, fun, cute kid; despite his complex needs. We somehow had the naive audacity to think that if we just raised him with loads of love, his life would be fine. As it happened, our journey with him was one of God's greatest gifts. We learnt about the depths of pain and sorrow in the midst of incredible joy.

Metus' Mum was mute, unable to speak, and no one knew who his father was. Metuakore literally means no father. He was eventually known by his nickname Metus or sometimes 'Tin Man' because his face was often stained silver from sniffing solvent paint to get high.

Metus came to live with us when he was 11years old. In that first year we began to realise that the cute (big) little guy we loved may have more than just drug issues going on. He would go through periods of seeing things that weren't there and believing he had certain special powers. Initially we thought was quirkiness and kind of cute. But by the time he became a teenager though, we realised this was actually some sort of psychosis. Halfway through his 13th year he was admitted to a psychiatric ward for a few weeks. After being released he was still too unwell to go back to school. At the time Ash was working for a church organisation and also guest lecturing at various theology colleges. Metus would go with Ash to all his lectures and meetings and would spend hours typing out nonsensical stories on a typewriter we had given him. He still managed socially, going out with his uncles and cousins and mixing with the other foster kids we had living with us at the time. But we were also aware that his world was getting darker and more complex as we watched some of his childlike joy disappear. On 28th December 1994 our housemate Lisa received a knock on the door while Ash and I were out. An older Greek man and his daughter had come to collect Metus as his girlfriend, Denise was in labour. This came as a complete shock to us! Metus had just turned 15 a few days before his beautiful daughter Christine was born.

Loving Metus, and attempting to care for him, completely changed our view and understanding of the world. Ash often used to compare Metus' life to Leo Di Caprio's character in the movie Titanic. In that film, Jack meets Rose who is living life on the top deck with affluence and privilege and the world seems to work just fine for her. Jack is from below deck and takes Rose there to show her a different side to life. Metus and his struggles took us below deck. This is when our young belief that life is pretty fair for everyone, was shattered. We saw how the mental health system was failing so many families. Even with all our contacts and education we failed to get Metus the help he desperately needed. There were moments of joy, love and fun amongst that chaos. But, when the Titanic hit the iceberg, inevitably the poor were locked below deck so those on the top could be saved. Even as I write this I see it's what's happening in society today. I hear the metaphorical tapping of the poor trapped 'below deck' to protect the wealthy and elite.

Eventually, after a few years of darkness and desperation – in and out of youth detention and psychiatric care (even living in a tree next to our flat for a few days) – we hit our Iceberg. Shortly after his 18th birthday Metus somehow escaped from a locked psychiatric ward and was soon found dead from a chroming overdose. (Chroming is substance abuse by inhaling solvents or other household chemicals to get high. Also known as 'huffing', 'sniffing' or 'rexing'). There was no happy ending. No miracle transformation. No last lifeboat. Just death. Metus was our Jack. We didn't succeed in changing him. His life seemed to get worse the more we prayed. He however, changed us forever.

As a Christian, I long for 'Miracle A' type stories where a tragic life is changed and restored and there is a great outcome to share. Mostly however, I experience type 'Miracle B' type stories. These are the ones I pour my life into trying to help others, then their struggle and tragedy transforms me irreversibly. I get to see how the world really works for the majority of people on earth, not just the privileged few. I can't un-see it and there's no going back. Rose can't go back to her top deck life either – as much as she tries – she is forever changed by the world Jack has shown her. When tragedy hits, the poor are quickly sacrificed so those on the upper deck can survive. The world continues to be this unjust place that exploits the already broken so that those in power can continue to thrive. At Metus's funeral, which still haunts me today, Ash and I made a promise – that we would devote our lives to fighting the poverty and injustice that was so much part of his short life. His beautiful daughter Christine is an amazing bright light who shines all the best bits of her dad, and our work ever since that tragic day is Metus' legacy here on earth.

Chapter 13 – Hope in the Time of Corona

Winson Green, 2020

"Week four of pandemic lockdown begins today. Strangely I have quite enjoyed the change of pace and the chance to stop regular activities and re-evaluate. I definitely enjoy change, and in the midst of this uncertainty, I am feeling really grateful for the way we live our life. Being locked down with eight people (only two of whom I'm related to) is actually quite fun at times. But I can't help but worry about all those we know and love who are stuck indoors in far from ideal circumstances, and the toll this is taking on already fragile mental health. What lays waiting for us all when the world reopens and a tidal wave of pain and stress flows out of the already kicked in doors?"

The worldwide coronavirus pandemic has hit the UK hard. Who would have thought that something like this could happen? The economic structures that we in the West have relied upon more than God are collapsing after months of shutdown. No one knows what the world will be like when we eventually come out of this. Unsurprisingly, the Titanic springs to mind again. The poor and disenfranchised have been shut away, literally, in appalling conditions. It is one thing for me to complain about being locked up in my lovely vicarage with ample room and a huge garden. But my neighbours are cramped into tiny, overcrowded rental houses, with dangerously substandard facilities. I can see them from my window, surrounded by concrete and rubbish. Worse still is the situation of our neighbours who have been housed in Houses of Multiple Occupation (HMOs). People sharing a roof with complete strangers many of whom have just been released from prison or mental health wards. We call HMO's 'jails without wardens'. Shared residential properties with 'common areas' that have been subdivided from single-family houses. Poorer neighbourhoods in the UK, like ours, are full of this type of accommodation. But even their distress bears no comparison to our Thai friends in Klong Toey locked down in tiny tin shacks during the hottest part of the hot season. Thousands of people surrounded by their neighbours; less than a metre away. The gross inequality of this world and the rhetoric-reality gap feels evermore present to me.

This lockdown period has highlighted the urgency of the problems we have been battling for 6 years here in the UK. Begging the authorities to change the disastrous systems that set people up to fail again and again. Asking questions about a structure that is punitive at the very time people most need support. To look at the hostile environment created by bad social welfare, housing and immigration policies.

In the midst of this challenging time, we have also witnessed precious moments. I am sure the same is true in communities all across the world. Gratitude is a powerful force. And people who assume they will be forgotten and overlooked, are so appreciative of even a socially distanced doorstep visit and hot meal delivery, that they in turn reach out to help others with the little they have. The 'neighbourliness' that so called modern society had almost sought to extinguish, is suddenly the way forward. On the news I am struck to see a group of care workers camping in tents. Choosing to sleep in the garden of the care home they work in to keep their patients safe from Covid-19. They camped like that for 12 weeks! I can't imagine the risk assessment and the safeguarding hoops that previously would have existed to prevent this. Yet those things seem to not matter in this crisis. Maybe we are finally more intent on helping others than worrying about correct protocols or being sued. Neighbours are cooking food at home for distribution to those who are self-isolating. No one is trying to them shut down an 'unregistered kitchen'. No one is checking their food handling qualifications. This is simply love in action. It is a welcome antidote to the global panic. It seems that love really does help to drive out fear (the Bible: 1 John 4:18). At a time when it would be reasonable to expect an avalanche of anxiety-fuelled self-preservation, I am seeing a revival of loving neighbourliness. I am filled with hope that perhaps the 'new normal' might include back-to-the-basics loving our neighbour. Serving others without being crippled by the illusion that security can be accomplished risk-free.

Hope has not always been something I am good at. But as I get older I realise that the panic and anxiety, that has peppered so much of the last 30 years of my life, has never got me anywhere. If I could write to my 21-year-old self, I would beg her not to take herself so seriously. To be less judgemental. Finally, I would plead with her to hope for herself in the same way her 50-year-old self has hoped for others.

Chapter 14 – Same Same but Different

Winson Green, 2017

I've got a numb bum from sitting through yet another safeguarding refresher training day. Now three years into my role working at a school in Birmingham, I'm resisting the boredom-induced urge to point out that the increasingly complex reporting protocols aren't actually working. It's the same every year and last year more children than ever were taken into care. But instead of getting myself into more trouble, I'm using the time to fret about two little kids down the street who are being left home alone (yet again) while Mum gets high. The under-resourced social services team have closed their case AGAIN. I am mentally rescheduling my diary, so I can take them to my house over the weekend to try and show them a little love and care. Hoping that by giving Mum a break it may give her enough emotional space to help her to accept the help she so desperately needs.

I've found that many parents in the community are scared to admit that they are struggling for fear that their kids will be removed. So instead, they suffer alone in silence, covering up their problems by isolating themselves and their children from anyone who might notice something is not right. But the sad truth is that we continue to witness families in dire situations slipping through the cracks of the system and being left to struggle in solitude.

Over the years, in Australia, Thailand and Birmingham, Ash and I have had lots of men, women and children stay with us. We have always tried to model what stable family life can look like. (Yes, I can hear you laugh! Me? Stable?) But, in my years of social work, I've observed that what people in crisis need most is a good friend, a supportive extended family network. Someone who will babysit for them, help pick the kids up from school, drive a strung out parent to mental health appointments, listen to their fears and go on fun outings with them. Public services are stretched beyond their limits, so reporting concerns up the chain simply isn't enough. Policies

66

and procedures can lure us into a false sense of security in thinking that our only responsibility is to make an anonymous phone call – then forget about those vulnerable children. We hope that someone else, who has been properly trained, gets around to dealing with it. We have a responsibility to those children who can't help themselves, to do more to keep them safe, and allow them to live out their God-given potential. Even in an ideal world, where the statutory support system is functioning efficiently, where families are rapidly visited by competent caring caseworkers offering sensitive interventions; those structures cannot offer love. Many times I feel I have no love left either; but I feel compelled to try. In Birmingham, I have met some amazing people who do this in a way that makes a real difference. Gwen Gardner, a retired nurse, is one of those people. Instinctively she just knows when a hug is needed or when a tough word is required. Gwen has loved so many people in our neighbourhood back to life. If you come to our centre, any day of the week, you will see a queue of people waiting to see her for help. She helps with anything she can, from benefit and housing forms, booking doctors appointments, setting up video calls with their overseas family members and much more (Nothing is outside her remit!). In my own messy way, I try to emulate her – making lots of mistakes along the way. But to be family to those who don't have supportive relatives around when they most need them most; is an honour and a privilege.

This sounds all noble. But the truth is that there is always something 'in this for me' – and my family too. I'd like to be all Christian and say I give without expecting anything in return. However, what I get back is a beautiful diverse eclectic network of the most amazing people. The privilege of having Pi Sim, Blah and Poo's families as part of mine in Thailand and now Ruth, John, Gwen and their kids as part of my extended family here in Birmingham is something I will be eternally grateful for. I get a deep sense of joy and comfort knowing there are people that have my back. People who I can always rely on and who my children see as their aunties and uncles.

One special woman is Ruth, the single mum who became one of our first friends when we arrived in Winson Green. She has been through a lot in her life and still trusted me – even when I was, at times, wholly untrustworthy. She has had to forgive me again and again for my big mouth. And I'm lucky enough to have the joy of having her three gorgeous kids in my life as a result. When I felt I would need to shut the youth group down as I couldn't find any leaders to help, it was Ruth who volunteered. Every Friday night she showed up to co-lead a drop-in club in our living room. This kept 20 kids off the street (and out of trouble). She then went on to run it entirely without me, gathering a great team of volunteer leaders around her. Ruth was nominated to go on the Urban Change Makers personal development course, run by Ash and his team. She was supported to set up a twice-weekly after-school club where children have a safe space to do crafts, homework and have a hot meal. The Newbigin Kids Club has now run successfully nearly every week during the school term for two years allowing 50 kids to attend. Last year she was asked to start another branch for a second school we work with; also proving to be a great success. We recently secured grant funding to pay her part-time hours for the work she was already doing for free. After receiving her first pay check in 10 years, she messaged me saying: "Thank you for seeing in me what I could not see in myself." Even when we are struggling ourselves, we have something to give our community. Giving whatever we have and being connected to people who care, can be so healing. I realise now, that when we hit hard times, we don't need an expert to tell us what to do – rather we need the love of good friends. The friendship Ruth offers to so many women struggling in our community is precious. Ruth continues to uncover people's gifts in this community, and this week I had the joy of being able to offer paid employment to one of Ruth's amazing ladies.

Chapter 15 – Neighbourhood Watch

Springvale, 1994

I am freaking out. Her hands tightly grip my arm and I can feel the cold tin of the garage door press corrugated ridges into my back. I feel that any moment I might be lifted off the floor. Shaking with fear and silently screaming 'God help me', she's not letting up.

After the Springvale youth centre burnt down, we started developing more neighbourhood youth programmes in various deprived neighbourhoods around South-East Melbourne. Ash and I also felt we wanted to move to a less 'posh' area. We were fostering two Vietnamese boys, Vu and Minh, along with Metus and his cousin Anthony, so it made sense to move to Springvale near their families. When we took in Anthony, to ensure he could get youth homeless allowance, I wrote a social work report detailing the violence he suffered at home (which led to his homelessness). But, on the way to hand in the report at the Job Centre (Centrelink), he had visited his sisters' house. When they read what I had written about their father they were furious. They called me over to talk about it and I soon learnt the hard way to never visit two angry Pacific Island women on your own! By some miracle though, I went from being held up against the garage door one moment, to sitting together on the sofa while they poured their hearts out, the next.

We cried together and talked about a dream of a different way of life. The result was that these two girls moved into the house across the road from us, and together we started a small church. Ash and I believed in local people having full say and control over the things that they start. So when they named it Whakka the Whanno (pronounced Fukka the Fano) we went with it despite the many raised eyebrows from within our church denomination. Eventually we convinced everyone to refer to it as Fano and Friends!

Anthony's sisters lived in a house for girls' we developed by renting a home across the road. We had also taken in a Cambodian foster daughter and – given the age of the teenage boys living with us – we thought separating the houses would be wise! Over time the neighbour over the back fence joined our little group with her children, and we decided to knock the fence down (it was falling down anyway) and make one big shared back garden. One night there was a big commotion. The police arrived and were running around with torches. And that's how we discovered that the cars that kept showing up in our neighbour's garden were not ones her brother bought to 'do up and sell' as we had been told, but rather stolen cars that were being chopped, resprayed and sold. It was also about that time that we discovered that our lovely, studious Vietnamese foster sons were working for a major heroin trafficking gang. Each time we dropped them at the library it was not to study – but to meet customers and sell drugs. To say we were naive was, and probably and still is, an understatement.

Sadly, conflicts within our little group and a few more incidents, where I was threatened with violence, resulted in my first ministry-induced breakdown. In retrospect, I see this was the only way I could start to learn about who I really was. To examine my motives for spending my life helping others. Obviously, falling apart by having an emotional identity crisis is not ideal. But it did create an opportunity to rebuild and come out stronger. That was the case for me. Back then, emotional meltdowns were most commonly referred to as 'burn out'. That label was sometimes spoken of as a bizarre badge of honour in some Christian circles. I don't like the romanticised idea that breaking down is some kind of missionary medal; but I do believe God can use our dark times to shed light.

During my first 'dark night of the soul' experience I learnt that not only was creating a community difficult, actually it was not what we really wanted (or were able) to do. A wise friend said: *"Community should be a by-product of a common mission together – not a goal in itself. When it is the focus, community self-implodes as self-serving introspective work and never survives."* So we gave up on trying to manufacture a community. Instead we focused on driving our shared mission of encouraging neighbours to use their gifts towards transforming our neighbourhood for the better.

When we later looked back we laughed because we had indeed attracted a strong team of comrades and a healthy sense of community along the way. Just knocking down a garden fence could never have achieved all that.

Our naive and overly optimistic expectations of communal living had been shattered by harsh reality. After picking myself up off the floor (literally and metaphorically), I slowly got over the shame and disappointment of it all going down the drain. I was ready to let God show me a new plan.

Chapter 16 – Anxiety Overdrive

Klong Toey, 2010

My heart is pounding so hard it feels like it is punching me from inside my chest. I hold my breath and my mouth fills with saliva. The shining metal of machetes glimmer as they catch the sunlight. We run into the house, but I can still see the violence through gaps in the wall of our tin house. The thump and thud of Machetes hitting a body is a sound I can't unhear. In slow motion the commotion dies down. Carefully we all emerge from our hiding places. A young man is bloodied and crumpled on the dirty ground, but amazingly, still alive. He is thrown on a motorbike and taken off to hospital. Aiden and his friends go back outside and keep playing as if nothing had happened. But I can't stop shaking.

Tempers often flare in the humid heat of the cramped slum shacks. Violence is a daily reality and each year a number of deadly fights break out. On this particular day my worst nightmare unfolded in front of my eyes. I stood frozen to the spot as it kicked off right in front of seven-year old Aiden and his friends playing with rhinoceros beetles. I swiftly grabbed them all and whisked them into the house; but not before they saw violent blows landing on the hapless guy a few metres away.

I have always had a deep fear about those I love getting hurt. Especially after having kids. People often observe my life choices and assume I am fiercely brave. But in truth, the reality is quite the opposite. Witnessing this attack left me badly shaken. Thankfully this young man survived, but only to go on to be killed just a few months later. He was tragically stabbed to death in the middle of afternoon in front of another group of tiny kids. They came running into the house to tell me, describing the events in awful gory detail. For days afterwards the five and six-year-olds could be seen acting out the scene and laughing as if it were all just a funny game.

After our daughter Amy was born, while we were still living in Springvale, the post-partum hormones sent my anxiety into overdrive. I couldn't do simple tasks like fill up the car with petrol. I had to plan everything over and over again to avoid things I found scary. When we drove past a woman being beaten up on the side of the road, my friend Lisa jumped out of the car to help her, but I sped home to call the police from a safe distance (no mobiles back then). Maybe that was sensible, but I looked at Lisa and wished I could be as brave as her.

Eventually I joined a peer support group called GROW. It made a huge difference to my mental health. It turns out there are hundreds of people who suffer similar struggles and I have found that being open and honest about whatever our problems are really help. That secrets lose their power when they are brought out of the shadows into the light. I also think, for me, moving way outside my comfort zone to a slum in Thailand actually acted as an extreme form of exposure therapy. I was either going to get better – or die – from sheer panic.

One such day Blah's brother-in-law drove us in his pick-up truck along with 16 other people a table and a TV. I vividly remember clawing my nails into Ash's arm as he hit 150kms per hour on the motorway. To make matters worse, six-year-old Amy was in the back of the truck singing and laughing with all the other kids. I was struck mute by my inability to even speak enough Thai to ask them to get her in the cabin. I prayed for a quick painless ascent to heaven when we crashed, but somehow, we all survived unscathed. Although, I did avoid getting back in that truck whenever possible.

The slum is a world of real danger. But life is lived intensely amongst all the fragility and death. Strangely, I've actually been more scared about my children's safety since we left. In Bangkok, I used to drive my kids to school on a Motorbike scooter with bare legs and flip-flops. Now I worry about Amy so much more far away in the supposedly safe suburbs of Melbourne Australia.

What is interesting to me is that since I have been living back in the UK I have felt the anxiety gradually creep back and take a hold again. Is there something about how wealthy modern society is structured that is not healthy for me? For any of us? Anxiety seems to hang like an unwelcome cloud over my life, and I'm sure the combination of menopause and a global pandemic have not helped!

I spend so much of my time worrying and trying to keep my kids and myself safe. Yet I know this world is a dangerous and often tragic place where terrible things happen to good people all the time and stressing offers no protection. We are fooling ourselves if we think we are in control. What I do know is that God is there in the middle of it all. And life is only really worth living if it's done wholeheartedly!

The bible says: "Therefore I tell you do not worry … Can any one of you, by worrying, add a single hour to your Life? (Matthew 6 v 27)"

But that is *so* much easier said than done!

Chapter 17 – Vulnerabilities and Secret Imperfections

Springvale, 1997

Sweaty and breathless, the stress has given me a headache. I'm supposed to be helping Laurel lead chapel in the women's prison, and I am running embarrassingly late. Trust me to lock Amy in our car on the way to taking her to stay with Grandma. I had to wait ages for the RACV/AAA to arrive and unlock the door. They better not report me to children's services!

Right from the start of my social work career, I knew I wanted to support women. Especially those who faced losing their children to the care system. When Amy was born I started volunteering with an amazing person called Laurel Gore. She is a true unsung hero who is still serving women in prison to this day. Working with Laurel I learnt so much. She modelled the most committed, compassionate life and inspired me profoundly. I wanted to be just like her. I was faced with the reality that so many of the women leaving prison had nowhere to go. We had a spare room at our place, so it just seemed logical to invite them to live with us until they sorted themselves out a bit. These women faced lots of complications in their lives and had been through things I could never imagine. But we often found common ground in parenthood as I was figuring out how to look after my own young daughter at the time.

When I first met Rosie, she was a new inmate only two weeks into a fairly long sentence. Feeling understandably distraught, she went to see the visibly pregnant prison counsellor. Rosie explained to me how she had tried to strike up some kind of rapport during the awkward introduction by asking when the baby was due. The counsellor responded in cold voice: "I can't discuss personal matters with you." Poor Rosie left the room feeling ten times worse. She felt humiliated and not even worthy of small talk. Shortly after, she decided to go with some other women to chapel. Probably more out of boredom than spiritual quest. This was the day I rushed in late. Waffling apologies and telling the women how I had locked my daughter in the car. I barely remember that day, but many years later, when Amy was 17 and really struggling with life we met up with Rosie. She unexpectedly said: "I want you to know that I am now the AOD (Alcohol and Other Drug) team manager at a large Charity. I found faith and got my shit together through you and Laurel." She told the story of the encounter with the counsellor and how I came running into chapel blurting out my lunchtime drama. She said, "When you told us all how you'd locked Amy in the car I realised I can be real in the chapel. I thought to myself, 'These chicks are honest and down to earth'. As a result, I kept going and Laurel supported me in getting my life together." She then turned to Amy and said: "Your mum accidentally locking you in the car helped save me." We laughed about it, but I think something special happened in Amy's heart that day. I'm so proud to say that Amy is now a mental health worker devoted to caring for men and women with severe mental health and addiction challenges. The nice finale to the story is that in 2019, Amy also found herself on one occasion volunteering in the women's prison led by the amazing Laurel Gore and her Prison Network team. (As I am editing this story I can't help but get goose bumps. Minutes ago I received a message from Rosie saying this *"Anji Barker, you are one of the good ones! Real and Normal. How do you do it with a Christian head and heart?!"* I look at the message above and realise the last time I spoke to Rosie was 7 years ago when we met for the above story. I have no idea what has prompted her to make contact today- but can't help but feel God might be telling me to keep going and get this book finished!

Self-consciousness about our vulnerabilities, secret imperfections and embarrassing failures can keep the stories that build trust, the stories that create empathy, locked up inside us. I think it's actually been my mistakes and mess-ups that God has used most. When I look back at situations I was most conscious of, worried about, or directed the most angst-ridden energy towards – they were not nearly the most significant points of impact. Conversely, it's almost always been the small, barely remembered, throwaway moments of transparent vulnerability that seem to have made the most difference.

Chapter 18 – Designer Vagina

Klong Toey, 2013

Groggy and dazed after coming around from anaesthetic, I wasn't sure if I was dreaming. The nurses are in my room setting up a DVD player. The doctor comes in smiling and rubbing his hands together. He tells Ash and me the hysterectomy has gone well and he is now going to show us the DVD of the whole operation! We quickly decline – it's the last thing we need to see!

The joys of getting older. I had a partial hysterectomy in a very posh international hospital in Bangkok. It was a shocking lesson in the stark contrast between the treatment I received with private health insurance (as a foreigner) and the treatment my poor Thai neighbours receive (sometimes even from the same doctors). I had a top surgeon, a private room like a hotel, and nurses in droves each specialising in a different thing. One pair to check my blood pressure and temperature, another pair to administer medication and yet another nurse to support the doctor. One of Thailand's top income streams is cosmetic surgery. Many tourists come to Thailand on a holiday to get a nose job, breast implants or even a sex change. The surgery plus a few weeks recovering on a tropical beach all cost less than just the surgery in their country of origin. This hospital is known as one of the best for these procedures.

On the second day I noticed, in addition to my keyhole surgery sites, I had stitches down below. I asked the doctor about this. His swift response was: "Oh yes I removed some skin tags and tightened you up inside while I was operating. It's much better for your sex life". I looked over at Ash in shock. After the doctor left it started to dawn on me that I had had three procedures. Only one of which I had consented to. He had given me a three-for-one-deal. I remember thinking maybe I should have watched the DVD after all, as I was way too embarrassed to ask the details.

A few days later I came back to the slum to recover. When I was strong enough I walked a few doors down to buy drinks at a little house-front shop. The usual ladies were sitting around chatting in the heat of the day and asked me how the operation went. Known to be a bit of an over sharer, I told them about my surprise at having had the extra unrequested procedures. One of the women said she had seen that on TV and was wondering if she should get it done too? They teasingly inquired about whether the added-extra operation had been a success. I joked along and said I wasn't sure – but if you see Ash walking around with a big smile on his face you will know it was. Right on cue, Ash, who almost always walks around grinning, came walking down to the shop to get a drink. They all roared with laughter and in English I explained to him what had just happened. Ash was mortified at my oversharing and went home as fast as he could.

A few hours later, a woman wearing a Pahtong (Thai Sarong skirt) came to my door saying she wanted to show me something. Before I could stop her, she raised it up to her belly button. And there it was. An extremely prolapsed womb hanging down like an extra appendage. An extremely difficult and traumatic birth had left this poor woman disfigured. She was only 33 years old and had been suffering like this for two years. She assumed, with no money to do anything about it, she would be stuck like that for life. As a result, her husband rarely came home.

I wasn't sure what could be done but took her to my over enthusiastic surgeon for a consultation. The very next day he operated. Bless that weird and interesting man – he performed the operation and follow-up appointments for free, only charging me theatre fees. (I never asked her if she watched the video). I didn't see much of her after this, but I can remember her saying she felt normal and had no pain. I only hope her life improved as a result of the surgery. Even my inappropriate oversharing seems to have been used to help others. That's what I'm telling myself anyway!

Although I still wish I could be more reserved and think a bit more before speaking, I now know that being authentically me – warts and all – is okay. And at times has been a surprising gift in the communities that I have made my home. Being in Klong

Toey was a crash course in living authentically as there was literally nowhere to hide. There was also no room for pretence or performance with all the holes in the walls. I couldn't keep up a façade even if I'd wanted to. It prepared us for living in a shared house with others in the UK. It's a fast track to accepting that everyone knows all your faults.

Chapter 19 – Parenting and Plaster Casts

Klong Toey, 2003

I am completely in love. We have just brought our beautiful baby son home. I gaze at him – an adorable ball of perfection lying in his cot in the centre of our room. So vulnerable, so perfect – ten fingers on his tiny hands. Except, looking closely, I notice he already has a film of dirt under his fingernails. Ugh, of course he has. It's impossible to keep anything clean for long. There are semi-open sewers one metre from this room. There are cockroaches and rats all around, and the oppressive heat means he has tiny sweat beads on his nose. What am I doing bringing my precious children up here?

There's one question that always gets asked about our life in Thailand: how did your children cope growing up in the slum?

These are my children's stories to tell, so the real answers are still to be written. But, both Amy and Aiden have grown up to be amazing young people. I couldn't be prouder of them and the integrity with which they live their lives. Most importantly, they are good people who are fun to be around. Amy lives in Australia with her fiancé Rob. We miss them terribly being so far away. My dream is that one day we will all be in the same country again; perhaps even working together. Aiden has just started college. He is an intelligent and thoughtful young man who has a very mature and interesting outlook on the world. Although, for a while there, he was rebelling and becoming a right wing capitalist in his views! True rebellion when you have such lefty parents!

The hardest part about parenting in the slum was not being able to protect your children from the harshest parts of life. I hate that my kids saw such shocking things. Raw and real life happened around us. They grew up knowing how terrible life can be. But they also learned about resilience. They were surrounded by a community that loved them, showered them with attention and gifts and always protected them. Their childhoods were full of freedom and fun. But, no matter what we did to try and mitigate the risks, it was still a dangerous place for children. Dangerous, in fact, for anyone. Slum-dwellers are vulnerable to fires, floods, disease and violence. And we knowingly bought our blonde five-year-old princess to live there and stayed when our son Aiden was born. Klong Toey would be the only home Aiden would know until he was 10 years old. Even though his parents struggled to string a sentence together his mother tongue is Thai.

Once, when my mother-in-law was visiting, she came downstairs to ask what was the commotion outside. Aiden piped up: "Oh it's just someone stabbing someone again Granny!" My first thought was: *Don't tell Granny that! What on earth will she think?* And then it struck me as so sad that my little boy, that any little boy, would know that there was violence just outside the door and think it normal.

My struggle, that remains unresolved to this day, is that tens of thousands of children live there. Children with much less love and security than we gave our kids. Lots of people seemed very concerned – questioning me about the safety of my kids – but don't those other children matter just as much? Was it right that I brought my kids along with me while I tried to make a difference in people's lives? Or is that a White Saviour complex, carefully cultivated by my privileged upbringing? I struggle to know the truth. But what I do know is this: I'd rather have tried, and got things wrong, than to have not tried to help at all. Some people worry so much about saying, thinking and believing the right thing while never really doing much of anything to help in the real world. Those who are more gifted than I am, will discover ways of doing things better than I managed to. That is not something I fear. It is my heart's desire that another generation will rise up and model a healthier, more inclusive, deeply transformative way of living. I hope to follow their lead! But I personally couldn't just wait around for a perfect role model or a fool proof theory to appear before getting stuck in and giving it my best go.

One March I had to go away to a conference with the team. This meant an overnight stay in Northern Thailand. Ash was also away speaking in the UK. I packed up some bags for the kids to stay overnight with friends from school. I arrived in back in Bangkok on a bus after a rough overnight journey, picked them up from school and headed home. Alisha, my teammate was with us as we walked back into the slum. We heard the news that a little local boy, Orr had broken his leg. Orr was a tiny, dirty six-year-old boy who would come to our house to wash once a week and play with Aiden. He was one of many neglected kids in the neighbourhood and was in our community centre most of the week. Orr's mum was a seriously addicted glue-sniffer and was suffering the subsequent brain damage from many years of solvent use. She roamed around the community and often got into dangerous or compromising situations. While her Mother cooked and sold food to make a living, she was forced to chain her up to the fridge to keep her safe. Seeing any human being in chains is a sight that is very hard to cope with. But with two very active grandsons, no husband and a drug addicted daughter, Orr's Grandma was left with little choice.

When I heard Orr was hurt, my first thought was, I'll go and see him tomorrow. I needed to get my own kids settled, and I was dog-tired after the long bus ride. I got my two in bed by 8pm, then realised I needed to buy washing powder to clean their uniforms. Somehow I mustered the energy to get to the little shop house a few doors down where I saw one of Orr's relatives. They confirmed that he had indeed broken his leg and was in hospital. When I asked who had gone with him, I found out it was a 10-year-old girl. In hospitals for poor Thai residents, you don't get fed or cared for if you don't have someone with you. Furthermore, it's an extremely confronting place. There are people in all kinds of injured states – often laying in beds right next to terrified small children. Our local hospital, called Kluay Nam Thai, was particularly bad, and we called it Kluay Nam Die. If you were unfortunate enough to go there, the chances are you would never come out alive.

I went home and asked Alisha to watch my kids as we both agreed someone should go check on Orr. When I arrived at the ward it was like a horror movie. I could hear him screaming in pain. Laying next to him was an elderly road accident victim with a gaping head wound. I squeezed myself between the beds to get to him and as soon as he saw me he grabbed me and held on tight. "Take me home!" He cried: "It hurts." A large rudimentary lump of quartz rock hung on a string pulling his leg straight. More than seven hours had passed since he had broken his femur falling off monkey bars and for seven hours he had been mostly ignored. He was shaking with shock and pain while the nurses passed him by. I was furious and demanded pain relief.

The law in Thailand is that everyone is entitled to 30 Baht worth of free healthcare. This is about 50p. And at that time it did not cover pain relief. Not even for a six-year-old boy. Orr was now writhing in agony and gripping my arm, his eyes bursting with panic and fear. I immediately offered to pay for painkillers, and the nurse told me that they could only be administered when the doctor came back on duty the following morning. I couldn't believe it. I called Alisha for advice, and we decided to get him transferred to the private hospital where our family and the team all went. Fortunately, it was only around 2kms away, and when the ambulance arrived to transport him, they immediately administered morphine, took the rock off his foot and splinted his leg. Orr who had been shaking from the last seven hours of intense trauma, was now out of pain, smiling and even joking with me. Having no idea how much this was going to cost I started calling around to friends to see who had credit cards we could use if mine and Alisha's were not enough. We arrived at the lovely hospital, greeted by smiling nurses who looked like supermodels. They presented me with the bill as they wheeled him into the emergency room to the calming sounds of a man playing a grand piano in the foyer upstairs. It cost £50 ($100). I breathed a sigh of relief that quickly turned to anger as this boy suffered so much and it only cost £50 to prevent all that pain. The big bills however; were still to come.

A surgeon was called and x-rays were taken while Orr was happily chatting and asking inappropriate questions of the doctors and nurses attending to him. Kids in the slum are not introduced to what we might call the 'social niceties'. Meanwhile Alisha had located his nine-year-old brother Emm – effectively his carer – who arrived by motorbike taxi. No shoes, covered in dirt and oversized shorts hanging off his tiny hips, held on by a rubber band.

The doctor came to speak with me and said that Orr will need an operation to set his leg in a Spica cast. This whole process at that hospital would cost about 160,000 baht (about $6000/£3000). I explained that the family had no money and asked what the alternatives were. Basically, without the operation, he would need to go back to the terrible free hospital and lay in traction for three weeks. I couldn't imagine sending him back there and immediately went into overdrive thinking of where I could get this money from. I had a community medical fund that was used to help children and adults in desperate situations. But this was more than the whole year's budget! And even if we had those funds how could I justify spending it all on one person? I excused myself and started calling around to get advice from the team. During that time Orr and Emm had been sharing their life story with the Orthopaedic Surgeon. When I hung up the phone, he came to me with tears in his eyes. He said he would like to do the operation for free. I would be left with a bill for the theatre and nurse costs – which was only a few hundred dollars. But the deal was he wouldn't be admitted to hospital and I would have to nurse him myself at home. I quickly agreed to this and they went ahead. Unfortunately, my Thai was never as good as I thought. I had no idea that a 'Spica cast' is not a normal leg-in-plaster-and-crutches scenario!

When they brought me into the recovery area to see him, I had such a shock. He looked like an Egyptian mummy stuck sitting permanently upright, plastered down both legs, with a bar firmly fixed between to hold his hips at a right angle. Oh my! I was starting to panic. We had a tiny home with a squat toilet – how would we ever cope? I felt God whisper in my ear: "Calm down you are going to look after him just fine". It was now 4am, and I was beginning to wonder if I might have hallucinated the whole thing. With no idea how this would work, I took him home at 5am.

Apart from the obvious difficulty of dealing with a boy covered in about 10kgs of plaster in 38degree heat and no proper facilities, the hardest thing was the criticism we (and Orr's Grandma) were subjected to. The local women made no attempt to hide their loud views that taking a boy in a wheelchair into our house would bring bad luck to our family. They were highly critical of Orr's Grandma, and no apparent compassion for the fact that she already had her hands full trying to manage his mother, while cooking and selling food. I knew it was jealousy, mixed with animistic beliefs, that largely motivated the gossip – it didn't make it any easier to cope with. By the second night, the rumours, open criticism and lack of sleep got the better of me. I stomped outside and joined in the chatter trying to defend Orr's Grandma – and me. The women explained that Orr's family must have done something in their past to bring this bad luck to themselves, so we shouldn't interfere.

I explained that I didn't believe in luck: good or bad. That good and bad things happen to both good and bad people. That's just life. But, as a Christian, I am called to help others if I can. The ladies laughed and then lots of jokes were made about evil people that I should help as long as we didn't want to live long. Thais have a great irreverent sense of humour and I learnt to laugh a lot. Mostly at myself! Two days later, Aiden, aged 6 at the time, had his leg run over by a pick-up truck. The jokes about karma weren't very funny after that.

Because Orr had broken his leg at the beginning of the Thai summer holiday I had to take him, Aiden, his brother Emm and various others who wanted to join in the excitement, to the community centre while I worked. Later that afternoon the boys were all running around the concrete football pitch and I hadn't noticed them dump Orr in his wheelchair and run off to buy ice-cream. Suddenly one of the motorbike taxi drivers is running towards me, Aiden in his arms, saying he had been run over by a reversing pickup truck. So off we went, plaster boy in tow, back to the same hospital. And there were the same doctors and nurses on shift. I felt the need to clarify: "I swear to you I don't break six-year-olds' legs!" Aiden was given immediate pain relief, and despite the weight of the truck, he only had a tiny fracture. He had healthy bones, not malnourished like Orr's, so he had limited damage. The fact that I didn't have to worry about money in this time of stress, as we had insurance, also meant Aiden got the best treatment and avoided hours of pain. We were given a lovely extra large room for the night and I slept there with both boys and their plastered legs. It seems so wrong that, just because of the birth lottery, Aiden was able to receive such good care. Orr with a much more serious injury had suffered so much. So maybe I do believe in luck after all.

Now I had two boys in wheelchairs at home. The women were waiting on my doorstep when we arrived home. They wanted to make sure they could say 'I told you so'. They had warned me this would happen and I was too exhausted to argue. The next morning, feeling calmer, I joined them in their chatter, tried to explain myself and defend my beliefs. As was often the case in Thailand when our world view clashed – it was put down to *Farangs* (foreigners) being different to Thais. It's exhausting trying to understand and be understood; and not just in Thailand!

What I didn't realise was that another neighbour was listening to all this gossip. She had a secret. The secret was her 3year old granddaughter called Safe. Although she lived just a few houses behind us, we had never seen her. That was because Safe had been born with clubbed feet and hip dysplasia. In Thai culture disability is seen to be caused by karma – something you did wrong in a past life so carries with it great shame. The dishonour of having a disabled child, coupled with the lack of affordable services to help, means many children like little Safe are hidden away. Spending their lives inside tiny, cramped shacks and even tied up as they get older. But this lady had overheard my conversation with my neighbours and was interested that, even at risk of bad karma, I was still willing to help Orr. Later that night under the cloak of darkness she carried little Safe over to our house and asked if I could help her.

It took two years of operations, physiotherapy and many, many, doctor's appointments. It also took incredible generosity from amazing kind volunteers in Thailand, and generous donations from lovely people in Australia to pay Safe's grandmother a monthly wage to allow her be her full-time carer. This meant helping her do daily exercises and attending the many hospital stays needed. Amazingly Lyn, my friend and physiotherapist, who was helping me with Orr was also able to help advise and provide physio for Safe. She also raised funds from amongst her expat friends so that we could get her and Grandma the things they needed. Safe, now 14 years old, is able to walk because of these interventions. A few years ago I had the privilege of watching her run around at school and it made my heart sing. Stories of hope are born out of the saddest situations. Although I wish the injustices didn't happen at all.

As for Orr? His leg took almost 16 weeks to heal. The heat in the slum, combined with me dropping him and accidentally tipping him out of his wheelchair a number of times, meant the plaster kept cracking. His malnourished state meant his bones took much longer to recover.

The rest of the Fabulous Four: Cheryl, Nicole and Kirsten all helped care for these kids and many others. Many more amazing teammates, supporters and volunteers were working away in the background to protect them from preventable permanent disability. It truly does take a village to raise a child, and I have been so blessed with who God has put in my life to help me when the needs feel overwhelming. Aiden's memory of that time was – not only did he get a broken foot – he also got an annoying six-year-old brother! Those boys remained very close until we left Thailand four years later. A few years ago when Aiden was back in the slum visiting, he and Orr's brother Emm had an awkwardly shy but cute teenage exchange remembering some of their childhood exploits.

Chapter 20 – Exposure

Melbourne, 2013

"I grew up surrounded by rats, pythons, gangsters and prostitutes" by Amy Barker, 17 screamed the headline on the front cover of the magazine. I'm buying snacks in my favourite supermarket in Australia when I see a picture of our beautiful, blonde-haired, blue-eyed Amy at the cash register. I panic and buy all the copies I see.

Until she was 14, Amy loved living in Klong Toey. She had loads of friends, ran a little shop at the front of our house and spent her time playing and enjoying community life. But when she became a teenager, something started to shift. There was a growing disconnect between her wealthy friends at the International School she attended and her lifestyle in the slum. The tension started to take a toll. All teenagers like time in their own room; but hers was a tiny space in 38-degree heat. Rather than music she listened to the fights and raucous noise of the street outside her flimsy bedroom wall. When she was younger, she had found it fun to have her school friends over to sleep at ours. Once they painted our dog pink and a wall purple (That's what I call a memorable sleepover!) But she was growing up fast and starting to really struggle with anxiety.

By the age of 15, it was clear Amy was not doing well. The unwanted male attention in the slum was overtly sexual and made her feel shy and uncomfortable. Her closest friends in the community either had babies or had gone into sex work by the time they were 13. So her remaining connections were only her friends from the private International School. Underage drinking and drug use was common with expat kids. ID is not required to buy booze and kids from wealthier families are often left alone to be raised by maids and drivers with loads of money available to them. Some of Amy's friends were well into that scene and Amy seemed to be getting herself into this also.

We could see that living in the slum at her age was no longer fun and adventurous but rather scary and highly stressful.

Aiden, being 8, was still loving his life and friends and we felt caught. We tried a few things such as going away more and renting an apartment outside the slum where we would spend weekends. But Amy's struggle continued. Just before her 16th birthday, at her request, she moved back to Australia in time for a few months of Year 10 to be ready for VCE (equivalent to UK A-levels) the following year.

This was a really difficult time for us as a family. By then we had taken in two Thai foster sons who were without passports and couldn't travel. Aiden was assessed as having extreme dyspraxia and dyslexia. His school was providing 13 hours per week of one-to-one intervention which he needed and would not get at an Australian school. When we mentioned moving back to Australia, Amy threatened to drop out of school if we did. In the state she was in I didn't doubt she meant it. Some great people stepped in to help Amy at that tricky time. My older brother Nic and his family took her in and helped support her ,and then, early in year 11, moved in with some amazing young women in their 20s. She stayed there until Ash eventually returned to Australia a year later, followed by Aiden and I a few months after that. We were finally all together again for the last six months of her final year of high school and her 18th Birthday.

During those desperately difficult months there is one family that I could never have survived without. The amazing – and slightly crazy – Baxter family. Not only were they able to love Amy back to a healthy place that has helped shape her into the amazing woman she is today; they supported Ash and I, becoming some of our closest friends.

When teenagers go through life's challenges they need support but so often don't want anything to do with their parents. I believe this is why the Church can be such an important safety net. Our kids need to have other adults who will love and parent them when we can do nothing right. 'Aunty Lisa' was one of our amazing team mates and friends who, at times, without a thought for herself jumped on a plane from Sydney to Melbourne to be there when Amy was struggling. She also spent many hours calming Ash and I down and reassuring us that it was going to be ok.

But sadly, for Amy, the church community was not always so helpful and supportive. Propensity to gossip and criticise leaders' families without really knowing the details can be hidden under the guise of *"sharing"* or *"praying for"* people utterly devoid of actual compassion. Such damaging behaviour that adds to the Church's reputation as judgemental by onlookers. Equally, I think all parents of teenagers who are struggling, are acutely aware that their child's struggle is not their own story to share. Therefore, church leaders, and people in the public eye, are often the most isolated when they most need help and support. So we struggled to protect our children's privacy while barely keeping our own shit together.

I don't think church people are trying to be 'judgey' or self-righteous even though that is how it comes across. I think people respond out of fear and awkwardness. I wonder if we are – like my Buddhist friends – experiencing a deep unspoken relief that if these awful things are happening to someone else – then maybe we are not that bad. Maybe the bad stuff will skip over us …?

It was years later I learnt that Amy had misunderstood that our leaving the organisation we started and led for 22 years was because of her. I was so sad to hear that she had internalised and carried this false guilt and feel terrible that we were so unaware of this feeling in her. She immediately felt cut off from team members that she had previously considered family. As a teenager she thought she had done something to cause this. Over recent years, through social media, some have reached out to her. I love to see the excitement and joy this has given Amy and the reconnections have brought some healing from that terrible period in all our lives.

Just after Amy moved to Australia a magazine contacted her wanting to do a story about her life. We were nervous to say the least as we didn't know what she would say. But they were offering $800 for her story. At 16 the money was too tempting to say no. She agreed to do the article and I waited nervously.

There hadn't been a pre-release clause or chance to check it before printing. On the day it was published I was in the supermarket during a visit to Amy who was already anxious and up and down emotionally. We were both wondering how they would spin or sensationalise her story

When I read the article, I realised it was actually really beautiful. Amy had given a profound and moving reflection about the struggles of the poor. Even in the midst of her own struggles Amy understood life in a deep and – I think – amazingly Christian way. I realised that day she was going to be OK. Good friends were alongside her in Australia but the helplessness I felt as a mother of a teenage girl is something no one prepared me for. My heart goes out to parents who struggle silently assuming that everyone else is coping, when the truth is, being a teenager is hard, no matter how you are brought up. Watching your kids in pain and not being able to help is excruciating for every parent. I'm not sure any of us cope well.

Getting the right support is difficult for those who are looked up to as leaders. So we hide it and get defensive. Several of my friends have left their church and friendship circles feeling ashamed and worried that their normal but imperfect family challenges were being judged. This leaves people more isolated and alone to deal with struggles that many of us share.

Chapter 21 – Puke and Panic

Sydney, July 2004

I'm trying to ignore the voice in my head whispering: "My kids could have this all the time! This is what I have robbed them of by living in Thailand". It's July and we are sitting in the church creche. Amy is playing nicely with all the other squeaky-clean kids in her dainty dress. Aiden is wearing a baby grow for once. Back home in Thailand it's far too hot and humid for anything more than a nappy. He looks so cute and clean.

Aiden is 9 months old and we are visiting Australia to speak at supporting churches and to visit family and friends. My old friends, panic and anxiety have come back to visit. The way they did after Amy's birth.

Before we left for Australia, Bangkok's wet season had brought out the dreaded mosquitos and Amy contracted a second bout of Dengue Fever so bad that she had to be hospitalised. I was deeply troubled. Was I unnecessarily exposing my kids to illness and disease? Watching Aiden with beads of sweat covering his face while he lay in his crib, checking for signs that cockroaches were getting inside his net … it was hard to take. The power of parent-guilt, even in the face of strong calling and conviction, can never be underestimated or prepared for.

The next morning, we left that church in Sydney, and the lovely people there to fly to Melbourne to be with our family and teammates. On the plane Aiden started vomiting and had terrible diarrhoea. By the time we landed we had gone through every nappy and change of clothes in our possession. Thankfully his Granny and Oma didn't care that he stank, and were more than happy to hold him. The situation got worse, continuing through the night, and the next morning we ended up in hospital where he was diagnosed with the very contagious Rota Virus. Ironically, he must have caught it at the lovely clean crèche! He spent the rest of the week in isolation at the hospital but not before he had infected everyone who came to visit us that first day, grandparents included. Unfortunately, later in the week we were all at a wedding where it became apparent he had shared the love with our team mate, Lisa's little girl. She was a very unwell flower girl and Granny was still queasy. The Greek Orthodox priest decided he would like to hold the cute blonde boy, after the ceremony thankfully, and Aiden promptly vomited all over him.

It was grounding for me to be reminded that kids can get sick anywhere. It really helped to check my irrational guilt, always waiting in the wings, ready to overwhelm me. I also think it was the start of overcoming some of the unhealthy anxiety that I had picked up reading parenting books. Many kids in the slum, despite the inequalities they face, grow up healthy and often happy. I resolved to remind myself that my kids had a great start, and one of the world's best state-of-the-art hospitals was very nearby.

Parenting is hard. Wherever you are in the world. Being the parent of a 17-year-old teenager in the UK is not an easy task either. There is so much we can panic about and be scared of even in developed countries. At least in the slum I was a bit shielded from all the fear and pressure around GCSEs, A-levels, unemployment statistics and all the doom and gloom surrounding our kids. We are terrified that their futures will be ruined if they don't get the right marks at school. Of course there were risks and dangers in Klong Toey. But there were also benefits that I think easily outweigh the negatives. As a family in Thailand we were never lonely or bored and had a strong community around us to share most of our trials with.

Chapter 22 – Regrets, I Have a Few

Springvale, November 2016

My heart leaps seeing the photos of all the girls reunited. A strange mix of loving pride and crushing guilt whirls around inside me. I wish I had that time again, and even now it's hard to look at this picture without regret flooding back full force.

Over the past 30 years Ash and I have cared for around 40 kids. From new-born babies to teenagers, who, in the early days, were only a couple of years younger than we were. Sometimes we took in a mother and her children, and we looked after them all together. Other times for emergency respite care, to give a stressed out family a break from a particularly difficult child or teenager. Our foster son Metus made us foster-grandparents to the lovely Christine when he was only 15-years-old, and we were just 23!

One of the first mums to come and stay with us was Belinda. I was 21, and she was a year older than me. She and her two-week old baby came to live with us. She had been staying in a caravan on the front lawn of my boss' house (who clearly ignored the social worker professional boundary thing too!) But her relationship with the daughter's father had become violent. Baby Brooke was tiny and perfect, like a little doll, but sadly she was suffering the effects of methadone and heroin withdrawal. Brooke was the first baby I had ever held or looked after, so I learnt everything with her. (Sorry Brooke!) After a few days Belinda left us, disappearing one night back into the world of drugs and crime. We had Brooke with us full time for the next few weeks until mum was located and rehoused.

Over the following years, Belinda would come and go in various states of crisis. By the time Brooke was eight we had cared for her for a large chunk of her life. Belinda also went on to have a little boy called Beau and another super-cute little girl called Bonnie. Loving people with life-controlling addictions is a terrible heartbreak that affects the whole family. Belinda's family were a loving and caring one. Close at times, but then ripped apart by the chaos of her drug use and subsequent neglect of her children. We shared that journey with them. In some ways we had the easy and joyous part. We got to love these three beautiful children (who we called 'the three Bs'), making fun memories with them, taking them to parks, swimming pools, hosting birthday parties and tucking them up safe in bed at our home. There were good times being part of Belinda's extended family too. Happy memories – like when she decided to move nearby and got involved in our church. She decided she wanted to get married to her boyfriend and we celebrated their wedding as one big family. Ash's mum, Mary, turned up in her BMW to drive the bride and groom to her Aunty Nola's back garden where the wedding took place, Ash led the wedding service, and I was a bridesmaid.

But life was not smooth sailing for Belinda and her kids. Over the ten years we shared life together, Belinda brought chaos into our lives as we tried our best to love her. Initially I thought if we just care for her enough we could straighten her out. But eventually we realised we couldn't fix her and gave up trying. The best we could offer was to try and be a sign of hope for those kids and a consistent and safe place for them to stay. We could give them an example of stability and, maybe, in their future, this might help them break the cycle of poverty and addiction for themselves. We felt very real heartbreak whenever we sent them back home to a smelly house where drug dealers came and went. These precious little souls just loved their mum to bits and always wanted her no matter what. The emotional rollercoaster was a rough ride.

At times, we were the official, formally recognised foster carers for Belinda's children and other times, when we noticed things getting bad again, they could just stay for a while. As is often the case even today, Child Protection Services struggled to keep these at-risk kids safe, even with us involved. 10 years after we first met, a particularly harrowing situation occurred involving her desperate, dangerous boyfriend looking for drug money and we knew: enough was enough. So we sided with the child protection worker and shared some of what we also were concerned about the children not being safe. Belinda was furious.

The children were removed from her care and after that she no longer consented to them being placed with us. Those beautiful kids were the tiny victims of a terrible story and went through many years of hell moving from foster family to foster family. All this time Ash and I lived with remorse. We believed they must have felt we failed and abandoned them. I asked myself – why did I not just keep my mouth shut? Why did I not just let the chaos continue in our lives? But the truth is I was scared. Belinda had hooked up with a violent ex-boyfriend who had just been released from a long prison sentence. For no apparent reason they had both beaten up her previous partner, the father of Bonnie and Beau. He then understandably fled and cut off contact with the kids for his own safety. This new guy terrified me, and I was scared for Amy's and Christine's safety, who were four and six at the time. Nevertheless, it remains a huge, painful regret in my life. I wondered if they would ever forgive me. In our final year in Australia we did see Belinda and the children occasionally – at birthdays and events – but she would never let them stay overnight or trust me enough to tell me if she wasn't coping. That door had shut tightly. They ended up moving away from the area, and we lost touch when we moved to Thailand.

In July 2014, through the power of social media, all three of Belinda's children (and Belinda herself) contacted me. And later that year, when we were thrown our farewell party, Bonnie and Brooke came along with Brooke's three gorgeous children. Two years later we all met up again when I was in Australia. It was so great to see Amy reconnect with the girls. We stayed in touch after that and one of my favourite pictures is this one of Amy and Christine with Brooke and Bonnie in 2016. (Beau is living interstate working, an absolute miracle as neither his mum nor his dad had ever had a job. He has two children, and we occasionally hear from him.)

Belinda and I stayed in contact through Facebook occasionally messaging each other over a period of a few months until she died tragically, but perhaps not unexpectedly.

Like loving Metus, loving this family shaped who I am and how I see the world. By God's grace, any good work that I have been able to do since is a result of what I learned loving these beautiful kids.

… Brooke has informed me about a book that you are writing. I think it's fantastic that you have decided to do this. She has also told me that you have mentioned us in your book and I give you permission to use my name. I would also like to acknowledge everything you did for us, you, ash and your family have no idea of the impact you have put on my life personally, I'm nearly 28 years old and to my family and others that are interested in my story you all play a big part as I still speak about you all till this day. Every memory as a child going to your house was fun, loving, warm and love. I was always super excited to spend time with your family knowing were going to be fed, bathed, and loved. You all made a massive impact on my life that I will never ever forget. I'm sorry for the shit my mother and step father put your family through, which should never of happened to such kind people but you all never gave up which shows me there is some kind in this world. My children have heard every memory I have with your family and I tell them so they know there is always someone out there that will do anything to put a smile on a face. I wish you well with your book and would love a copy when it is finished! I still will never get over the fact you still help out when a couple years ago I put on social media about my unfortunate episode when I run out of toilet paper and you sent me a whole box full to make sure it won't happen again! I still tell people to this day it's hysterical!!! Hope you and the family are well and would love to see you all again and see the man I have become and meet my four beautiful daughters! Lots of love, the Clancy family.

Chapter 23 – Life Inside a Missionary Marriage

Klong Toey, September 2002

My husband is lying in a hospital bed. The round-faced doctor is smiling. It's not a reassuring smile. He's smiling too much. Thailand is called 'the land of smiles' for a reason and believe me when I tell you that not all of their reasons for smiling seem logical to a Westerner. This was one of those moments. "Not everybody dies of this!" he reassures me (smiling even more). "Not EVERYBODY" I scream in my head. Then how many!?

We have only been in Klong Toey for six months and Ash is sick, again. It's another bout of dengue fever. The worst sort, haemorrhagic dengue, the kind that makes your red cells break down so your blood can't clot. This puts him at risk of bleeding to death. I stare at my husband, drifting in and out of consciousness. He is really sick this time. The doctor is speaking again. "You will need to be very careful. Don't let him shave. A cut could be fatal!" Ash doesn't look like he'll have the strength to shave any time soon. "And don't let him get out of bed. He needs a bedpan." The doctor won't stop smiling. It's my birthday. I look down at my feet. I can see the same haemorrhagic spots starting to appear on my own feet. I have a banging headache – I better not say anything. Amy is watching cartoons on the couch next to the hospital bed and I need to stay well for her … so I smile.

When Ash and I met at Bible College, or *bridal college* as it is known, we knew we wanted to live a different kind of life. We wanted to go overseas to offer love to people who lived at the margins. We had both been influenced by American pastor, sociologist and social activist, Tony Campolo after hearing him speaking in Adelaide in 1988. We also read books, like 'Rich Christians in an Age of Hunger' by Ron Sider, and Jackie Pullinger's 'Chasing the Dragon'. We were keen to get married and get on with a life in full time service to humanity and God. We have been married now for 32 years. Ash likes to joke '29 happy ones'! I dare not ask which ones he thinks were problematic as I'm sure we may have a different take on that!

Some of our happiest times together were the early years in Klong Toey. Despite the dreaded dengue fever. It was just Ash and Amy and I having an adventure together. For a brief time, we didn't have a team to be responsible for. I think one of the blessings of being married to someone with a similar passion for ministry is that I have a comrade. Even when the rest of the world thinks I'm a bit crazy there's someone by my side who gets me. One of the pressures that has caused conflict in our marriage however, is those times when we are both equally invested in something and don't agree on how to proceed. As we have become older we have learnt the best way forward is to ensure that our work has some aspects of independence, and some overlap. Both of us need something we are passionate about that runs independently and some areas of work that we collaborate on – to complement each other. We could have saved ourselves some grief had we worked that out 30 years ago!

The pressure and heavy responsibility of emotionally draining work means that there have been times, in years gone by, when it adds strain in our marriage. These times it seems like pressure on our physical hearts too. Occasionally I have genuinely feared one of us might die of a heart attack. During those times I have longed for a quiet life ... before remembering it would kill me slowly and torturously with boredom. Even though Ash is more of an introvert he too only craves the idea of a 'normal' calmer life in short bursts. Although I suspect they are significantly longer short bursts than mine!

Thankfully we have always had good people around us who have helped us navigate difficult times. Life in Klong Toey suited me to a tee. I'm a natural extrovert whereas Ash is a high functioning introvert. I've learnt that I need lots of people to spread my energy between. It would have been impossible for me to live solely focussed on one or two people – it also might well have killed them! In truth, no one person can fully meet another person's needs. Ash and I have not always been great at letting each other be who we are, but as we get older, we have been better at encouraging each other in this way.

I learnt Thai more quickly than Ash, probably because he speaks one word for every five of mine, so I had more practice! I think I speak a lot out of a deep need for connection. In the places we have lived this has been a valuable gift, helping me to be a healthy version of my hyperactive self. While I immersed myself in our neighbours' lives at a pace, Ash was able to lean into his more reflective side, taking time out to read widely and write books. Which is why he has a PHD and has written 11 books, and it took a global pandemic to get me to finish writing my first book!

Ash's gifts have perfectly complemented mine. He brings depth and I bring the energy. When we are both in a healthy place we can really get things done together. I shudder to think how our marriage would have survived had we not embarked on this mission together.

I think there are real reasons behind why God encourages us to live in community with others. I am a lot to cope with even on a good day! Luckily for Ash there are other people to entertain my hyperactivity and plot my crazy ideas with. It's been especially important during these seemingly unending lockdowns in the Covid-19 pandemic. Being in lockdown and isolation with eight others has been a saving grace – although the others may now need therapy!

Ash really sacrificed those years in Bangkok. I think his writing and speaking kept him sane. I thrived and found exciting ways to explore gifts I didn't know I had. I think the UK is the reverse for us. I struggle to keep up with Ash and all his new ideas and projects. The cold weather really zaps my energy while it only seems to invigorate him.

It's interesting watching Amy and Aiden as they grow up, and seeing how in some ways they remind us of ourselves. Yet they have other aspects that are completely different and admirable. It's probably fair to say that Amy has turned out to be more like me (extroverted, hyper and very sociable) and Aiden like his dad (thoughtful, passionate with strong-held ideas and driven). Yet both have taken on the world uniquely. As I write this Aiden is planning to film a documentary about the Klong Toey slum. Amy meanwhile, is writing a course training mental health workers to run support groups. Something she has spent the last 2 years doing. We hope to give them both the support and space they need to grow into their truest selves and find roles that play to their strengths. While we find any excuse to brag about them!

Chapter 24 – Coming Out

Springvale, 2005

I look down at my jeans and feel super self-conscious that I'm the least glamorous person at the party. It's lunchtime and I have been invited to a BBQ. Aiden is toddling around winning friends with his cuteness and someone calls out "Anji, you don't remember me do you?" I take in the sexily dressed trans woman in front of me and slowly connect her to a faded memory of someone I used to go to church with.

Wherever I've gone in the world, I have found that people on the margins are often the most eager to help create compassionate communities. They know first-hand the pain of being excluded and oppressed. I had been honoured to be invited to this BBQ for older transgendered folk. When I arrived the host Donna, glammed up with some unfortunate blue eyeshadow, called out hello to me. I toy with the idea of suggesting a blending technique but – as the fish out of water – I decide to keep my mouth shut and just enjoy being a guest. As the day unfolds, men arrive, go straight to the bedroom and come out transformed (with varying degrees of success) into glamorous women. It was a lovely day. I was really welcomed and loved. I'm sure a stark contrast to how many of these lovely people would have felt if invited to a BBQ with some of my friends. I couldn't help but feel a real sadness at all the hurt these men experience and also for the hurting families they represent. For their generation double lives and secrets was the only way to be who they truly were. Given that the average age of the group was 40+ it made me hope and pray for a better world for young transgender people. Having friends on both sides of this story of secrecy and marginalisation, I'm aware it's a world of pain for all involved. Too often it's the church that is shovelling this pain in spades.

Since I was young, I have crossed paths with many people who identify as LGBT+. So I felt uncomfortable when the denomination our organisation was linked with became part of the "ex-gay" Exodus International Movement in Melbourne. I remember a friend crying her eyes out when she discovered her supposedly 'cured post-gay' husband had been caught having affairs with men. Sadly, even now, I continue to hear many stories about the collateral damage caused by this terrible and abusive therapy. I am continually surprised by the number of young people who were, and still are, kicked out of their churches and even their own biological families when they come out.

I have never been academic about theology. But I was trying to find arguments to counterbalance the readily available articles using the so-called "clobber passages" from the bible to preach condemnation. Even though in the early 90's I struggled to find any Christian writings that were not homophobic, I just couldn't believe in a God cruel and torturous enough to create someone with a sexual orientation they didn't ask for, then punish them as sinners for it. My sin is that I stayed too quiet for too long. For the next few years I quietly supported gay Christians and their families – many of whom are, or were, pastors. I was given lots of platforms to speak about God's heart for the poor and marginalised, about our work in the slum and the vision to see God's kingdom here on earth. But I'm so ashamed to confess that I never used those opportunities to speak up for my LGBT+ brothers and sisters in that context. I'm trying to make amends in these later years by coming out in public support now as often as I'm given opportunity.

Thank God, and the internet, in later years I was finally able to find sensible, sound theological explanations by respected Biblical scholars for those misused and abused passages. The misuse of these verses taken out of context has kept some of the most amazingly gifted people I know, from being allowed to bless the church with their gifts. I have tried to be a better ally ever since and, if I'm totally honest, the grace and forgiveness I have received from the LGBT+ community for my previous cowardly avoidance is stunning.

I'm from a generation that was not raised with politically correct terms. Someone often needs to take me aside to correct my language and explain why my statement is outdated or hurtful. I always find this intensely embarrassing but helpful. I spent so long being too scared to say anything in case I got it wrong. It's high time I just gave it a go and allowed a beautiful diverse group of amazing children of God to teach me. My corrective experiences have always been done with grace and kindness – very different to what they themselves have endured from people in the church community.

It has always made sense to me that we are 'created equal in the eyes of God' and that we should love and serve others. Why should beautiful, diversely gifted humans not be welcome to lead and serve? Why are we not encouraging LGBT+ young people to find the love of their life in a church congregation and be married surrounded by a community of faith committed to help their relationship blossom?

Recently I had the honour of meeting Harry who is 83 years old. He runs a support group for gay men. He is the youngest in the group and the only one who is 'out' publicly. The mental health issues and loneliness he deals with are extreme. These beautiful men were young and gay in a time when homosexuality was illegal and they faced a real risk of being put in prison. We are all horrified by that now – and that the church didn't just passively allow it to happen – but actively led the legislation under the Family Values flag to make sure it did happen! I wonder if our current Christian policy of being 'inclusive but not affirming' (welcoming LGBT+ folks to church but not encouraging them to lead, marry in our buildings or celebrate their healthy committed relationships) will be what our grandchildren are horrified by when they look back on us? Conditional love is not what any faith is about. Saying we love you but not the gay or trans part of you – is conditional and pushes young LGBT+ people into secret and unhealthy relationships that can damage their futures. We should be rejoicing with them when they find a loving Christian partner who wants to serve God with them. They should be given a chance to be mentored in a healthy marriage not forced to choose between celibacy or leaving their church!

I think God is tired of waiting for the church to wake up and lead on tackling this issues of injustice and, as has been the case with the issues of slavery and women's equality, God is using brave people outside the church to courageously drive this movement forward. I pray that eventually the church will catch up and treat all God's children with the loving acceptance they deserve.

Chapter 25 – Ladyboys

Klong Toey, 2006

Our visitors are a missionary family we recently met in Bangkok. As we sit on the floor in our little house having lunch, Amy and her Thai friends run in and out. Eventually the visiting children join in Amy's games. 12year old Anh comes in to borrow some of Amy's pink clothes. One of the visiting children whispers loudly to Amy, "Is that a boy or a girl?" Without thinking, Amy just shrugged and replied: "It's just Anh".

When we arrived in Thailand, I read up on 'ladyboys', or in Thai *katoeys*, in order to try and get a better understanding of why this well-known cultural phenomenon of a third gender is so prevalent. But my best learning did not come from books. What I discovered is that there are as many explanations as there are colours in a rainbow. One grandmother told me that she had too many grandsons. That's why the child is *katoey*. Another mother told me she beat her son whenever she caught him dressing as a girl. Some people believe children are born third gender while others believe that it's chosen by the individual. Some kids have their gender identity chosen for them. What I learnt from Amy, and from being immersed in Thai culture, is that the reasons don't matter. In order to love people; I don't need to understand which box they fit in. At some point growing up we seem to move from childlike acceptance of people as friends – without a thought to gender, race, sexual orientation or religion – to the need for labels and putting everyone into neat categories. For God's gorgeous creations, boxes will never be adequate.

Across the street from our home in the slum, lived two brothers (sisters) who both identified as third gender *katoey*. However, they had almost nothing else in common. Bon presented as androgynous, wore skirts but kept a moustache, cared for her elderly mother and never went out. Bang, on the other hand, had a boob job and became a successful go-go dancer. Amy's swift and beautiful response when questioned about Anh's gender showed how she fully accepted her friend without categorising their gender. Sometimes kids can be so breathtakingly wise. Thailand helped all of us see that God's creation is indeed far more beautiful and complex than Western labels have traditionally allowed for. The acceptance of gender fluidity is part of what makes Thai culture distinctive and vibrant.

In many ways, *katoeys* are accepted as a normal part of everyday life. They are often celebrated as the heroes of soap operas and known for being exuberant party-starters. It made sense that Amy enjoyed her loud and fun *katoey* friends. It's considered an honour to have a *katoey* dance for you, so some earn their money giving royal-assented dances at weddings and funerals. But the world is often full of contradictions and, even in Thailand, they are still the butt of jokes and exploited as sleazy entertainment for tourists. This is especially true for those from poor families. There's an intersectionality to being an outcast: rich *katoeys* are praised, poor ones; ridiculed.

Chapter 26 – God Loves All Her Children

Birmingham City Centre, 2019

I'm overwhelmed by the sense of unity and joy at Birmingham Pride. Standing in the street surrounded by glittery rainbow flags, this is the most profound worship experience I've had in years. I feel honoured to wear a "Christians at Pride" t-shirt again this year. The bubble is soon burst by a prejudiced Preacher screaming hate-filled messages about 'gays going to hell'. Suddenly, the LGBT+ Christians I'm with stop. It's like someone has hit a giant pause button on the parade and I wonder what will happen. Someone starts singing Amazing Grace and the whole crowd join in. The Preacher is love bombed and his hate filled speech drowned out with a chorus of redemption and God's love. The air is electric. It is a spirit-filled moment I feel immensely privileged to be part of.

In 2018 I was able to take part in Birmingham Pride March as part of Christians at Pride. I had the privilege, as an ally, to be marching with a group of incredible queer and straight Christians in our city. I was blessed to meet some amazing people through Christians at Pride none more special than local young power couple Lizzie and Naomi. These incredible women of faith have been a part of shaping our charity Newbigin Trust, and have inspired me so much. Naomi was the operations manager for our charity and a couple of others and is now co-CEO of Red Letter Christians UK (redletterchristians.org.uk) amongst other things. We are looking forward to celebrating their wedding this year. We know that God has got great things in store for their future as a couple of Christians committed to justice and love and making a difference in an unjust world. It is an incredible honour for me to be able to share life with some incredibly inspiring people of faith and my life is all the richer for the fact that many of these people are LGBT+.

The journey that led to Pride began after living eight years in Klong Toey. We took a three-month sabbatical to recharge, then felt ready to move to a rougher part of the slum called, Lock 3. Poo's cooking school was going great and she was booked out for months in advance. Together with Poo and some other neighbours we formed a social enterprise incubator called Helping Hands. Through it many new initiatives were formed: an ice-cream vendor, a Thai dessert trolley, a roadside coffee shop, a sushi delivery business and an online fresh-food delivery service; just to name a few. The Thai team in our neighbourhood was strong, and it was time to step out of the way a little. This gave me the energy and time to focus on something new. We rented a house deep within the new neighbourhood and that's where we lived for the next four-and-a-half years.

With the social enterprises growing, and many more customers from the expat community, I found myself with lots of email traffic and paperwork. Often I would have to be sitting up at night trying to get it all done after the boys were in bed. Pi Sim, my neighbour and her friend Noi, would sit outside on the step and often chatted to me about what I was doing. I was, and still am, pretty awful at technology and they could see me struggling. Especially when I needed to write things in Thai as well as English. Almost as a joke I asked them if they knew anyone who could read and write Thai but also speak English. Pi Sim said: "My daughter Kook can! She has graduated from university and lives with her girlfriend nearby. She is looking for a job." I couldn't believe it. Employing Kook made a massive difference in my life! We got off to a bit of a rocky start, but over time Kook's vision and gifts flourished. She became my PA and the General Manager of Everything! She would challenge me when my ideas were too Western. She understood life in the slum, and life outside it, and could interpret Thai culture for me. Working alongside Kook took me on a journey to better understanding of the life of gay women in Thailand. On one level, Thailand seems like a really open, inclusive place, but Kook showed me that the reality for LGBT+ people was far from that. On the surface Thailand can seem chilled and accepting of everything but the way people joke and raise their eyebrows – even about me employing a gay woman – says something. Interestingly in Thailand there are clearly assigned roles for gay women. One must be butch and masculine and the other feminine and petite. Kook and her lovely partner Tai don't really fit those prescribed boxes. This is so disturbing to people's preconceived ideas that on many occasions they are asked about this. It is always hurtful and Kook often asks: Why can't people just let love be love?

Kook is one of the most gifted and talented people I know. With her help we were able to register as a Thai charity and pay medical insurance and holiday pay to those that we employed through the social enterprises. That kind of thing is really complex in the West. But in Thailand with their love of mountainous paperwork: it is virtually impossible. During her time working with me Kook moved back into the slum community. She is still there continuing to support young women and children along with her mum and many nieces and nephews.

When we arrived in the UK, one of the first people we became friends with was Simone, a transgender woman and talented musician, well known in heavy metal music circles. After a break she had a passion to go back to her music scene. I remember saying to her, worried about old temptations of things that messed her up before, that she shouldn't do this alone – but as part of a team. One evening she called me and said she had taken that advice and signed both of us up to sell Terroriser magazine (the Metal equivalent of Rock's Rolling Stone) at the Damnation Music Festival in Leeds. It was totally out of my comfort zone and far from my usual taste in music. But I couldn't go back on my own advice and went along out of curiosity. I expected to see the stereotypical upside-down crosses everywhere, assuming the shouty goth musicians to be scary, angry people. But I could not have been more wrong. I met hundreds of softly spoken, sweet people who were up for honest conversations and welcomed me into their group with open arms. It did help that the other magazine sellers were also well known trans-women and many of the bands came and sat and talked with us. I felt I had been invited into the centre of a precious subculture. I also realised very early on that most people thought I too was a trans-woman. I decided that was a compliment and a redeeming feature of having vocal nodules all these years that makes my voice husky.

Sadly for Simone, the struggle for acceptance within the Christian community, was not as easy as within the metal community and the battle was too much. The toll on her mental health continues. As is the case for so many people LGBT+ people who find initial acceptance in the church and give their heart and trust to that community – only to find that there is a limit to how much they are actually accepted. Inclusion without proper affirmation is a damaging and harmful practice.

Looking back on this journey, I can't help but wonder what amazing opportunities have been lost to the church because we haven't welcomed and embraced all God's children. I know for sure our own projects would have been stunted and damaged if not for the queer people God brought into our teams. In truth, my LGBT+ friends and co-workers were *my* allies.

Chapter 27 – A Journey of a Thousand Miles ...

Saigon, 1997

It's Amy's first birthday! We're away on a two-week holiday staying with the family of our Vietnamese friend, Lavang. A chubby Catholic priest is playing his harmonica (badly) as Amy bounces on my knee gurgling with glee. She looks adorable in her traditional Vietnamese dress and squeaky shoes. Do we fit here? Is this the right place for us to be?

A question I commonly get asked is: how did we end up living in a slum in Thailand for 12 years? Looking back, I laugh at the messy way it all happened. But somehow, we just knew it was the right thing to do. The funny thing is that neither of us had any great passion for Thailand. I actually had my heart set on Vietnam. Three of our foster kids, Vu, Minh and Duat were Vietnamese and through listening to their life stories of struggle as refugee kids we developed a love for all things Vietnamese. (Although, if I'm honest, I never learned to like beef tendons or fish balls!) I went to Vietnamese language and culture classes and learnt about Buddhism, getting ready for when it was the right time to leave Australia and head over there. Working overseas had always been a dream but I was starting to wonder if it would ever happen. I knew I wanted to serve abroad but our work in Springvale was going so strong I wondered whether there would ever be a good time to leave.

We got the chance to dip our toes into Vietnamese life when we were invited by a friend from Springvale for a holiday to stay with her relatives. Lisa, our courageous colleague from Springvale, came with us. While we were there, we met up with a group called Inner Change. Their leader John Hayes, became a good friend. John is a wise man who helped us work out whether we were a good fit for Vietnam – and also what it might take to move there.

At that time, visitors to Vietnam had to stay in a registered tourist area. You had to hand your passports in to the area police.

Our whole purpose in visiting was to stay in a poorer part of town and see if it would be possible to live there in the future. Once the police heard where we were staying, we had to bribe them with gifts and money to let us remain. Ash has slightly Asian-looking eyes and was known as 'Lee Nguyen' when he played for a mainly Vietnamese football team in Melbourne. So we said he was a cousin of the family we were staying with. They had relatives who went as refugees to America and Australia so it was perfectly plausible. It worked for a while but eventually late one night there was a bit of a fuss and we got moved on into the official tourist hotel.

Walking around, we were surprised to see people queuing in the streets of Saigon to get into – of all places – church! Doubts about what we could bring to this country as outsiders started to stir within us. The more Vietnamese people we met and the many Catholic priests and nuns we spoke to made us doubt there was any need for outsiders, like us, moving in.

There was another flaw in our plan in moving to Vietnam. Everywhere we went, outside the tourist centre, we drew attention and crowds that caused our hosts trouble. Vietnam was still very strict in those days so, to truly support the poor living in Saigon, we felt there would be far more benefit in funding a local person who could move about more discreetly.

Our two weeks there was an amazing experience. I left a little early, not fancying taking Amy on the small plane required to visit Cambodia. But Ash and Lisa continued on to Cambodia and had a short layover, on route, in Thailand. Landing in Bangkok, Ash asked the taxi driver, "Where do the poor people live here?" and was taken (we found out later), directly to Klong Toey where we eventually lived. The taxi driver, fearing he would be robbed, refused to drive them inside the slum.

I was disappointed that we wouldn't be moving to Vietnam. All those language lessons wasted! But, with John's sage advice, we knew that it was the right thing to do and perhaps we would go there for a three-month sabbatical in the future. I felt ready now to get stuck back into work in Springvale. So we decided to recommit ourselves fully to our community in Australia for another five years.

I launched into new things in Springvale, joined the prison team with Laurel and set up a local 'Grow' mental health peer support group. Lisa was working for the mobile needle exchange giving clean syringes to IV drug users and so we got very involved supporting people struggling with addiction. We became part of a trial rapid heroin detox programme and invited some people to live with us during their rehabilitation. Looking back, this period of intense immersion in chaos and brokenness prepared us well for Klong Toey. Those years gave me more than enough opportunity to grow my gifts and put my hyperactive energy to good use. God sees ahead of the horizon and holds the whole picture.

About two years later, as Amy was turning three, we were preparing for our three-month sabbatical in Vietnam. The plan was that I would help at a children's home while Ash took time out to write his book Collective Witness. But a few weeks before we were due to leave, we were told that the charity I was to volunteer with had been refused permission to issue invitations for the visa we needed. Our plan was called off. We were gutted.

Thankfully Ash received a call from his friend Mick, who was working for AUSAID at the Australian embassy in Bangkok. When they were younger, Ash and Mick had toyed with setting up their own political party. They called it 'Christian Radical Action Party' or CRAP- the acronym left something to be desired! They were political idealists. Some would say socialists. They were going to run with a platform of zero unemployment. They figured, if everyone gave up a day of paid work a week and volunteered in their community, there would be enough jobs to go around and communities would be socially richer. (Mick followed his political passion into public service and continues to do incredible and radical community and political work.) He suggested we look at spending our three-month sabbatical in Bangkok. He had just been to visit an AIDS hospice, 'in

115

a large slum in the centre of the Thai capital'. He thought it would be perfect for us.

When we were eventually taken to the slum, Ash realised this was the same place the taxi driver had taken him on the stop-over two years before. We had arrived in Klong Toey. Never planning we would eventually live there and raise our children.

I soon started volunteering in the AIDS hospice and met a couple of other Westerners living there. An elderly Australian nun, Sister Joan moved there when she was 60 years old. She then spent 25 years living with and serving the people of Klong Toey. She remains a legend and one of my heroes to this day. While I volunteered, remembering the problems we had in Saigon, I asked her advice about the feasibility of our family staying in Klong Toey. She walked me straight over to Blah's house. As Blah could speak some English we eventually managed to negotiate a rental agreement. At first, she refused to help us. "You can't live here!" she said. She later explained that she was embarrassed by the living conditions and could not imagine Western people there, especially with a small child. We thought she just didn't want us as neighbours! But somehow, we convinced her and, a week later, moved in to spend our three sabbatical months living there. We hadn't thought it would be anything more than a three-month visit. Little did we know Blah's family would become some of our closest friends and that we would still be in touch 20 years later.

As we settled into our first taste of Klong Toey life, I began to see that the community was full of incredible women who battled each day to keep their families fed and clothed. During the three months that we lived next door to Blah's family her brother slowly wasted away from AIDS related illnesses. Frustrated at not being able to speak the same language I felt helpless that I couldn't console them – or even just pass the day chatting. Our room was directly next to theirs. Divided only by a plywood wall that had gaps at the bottom. During the night, our books would slide under the wall, and Blah's mum would come and return them in the morning. Like most people in Klong Toey our bathroom was a wet room consisting of a concrete tank of water to scoop over ourselves; and a squat toilet. When we were using it, we would leave a pile of our clothes and towel outside the flimsy plastic door as otherwise our clothes would be completely soaked. One morning, Blah's mother came over to return our books while Ash was in the washroom. He hurriedly threw a towel around himself, but as he reached down to take his clothes into the wet room to get dressed, the towel dropped exposing his white bum. Blah's mum giggled hysterically.

A day after the embarrassing towel incident, we were woken in the night by wailing through the plywood wall. We raced out to see what had happened; as had most of the neighbours. There was Blah's mum tragically lying dead on the concrete floor of a brain aneurysm. We tried to convey our shock and sympathy by facial expressions and soon realised we might be making things more difficult. So went back to our side of the partition wall, when Ash had a terrible thought. "What if the shock of seeing my bum killed her?" He asked me. Already feeling so awkward and unsure of what to do, we tried to stifle the inappropriate laughter that kept welling up. Shock can do that to people. Years later we told Blah this story and she laughed so hard she ended up on the floor.

Over the past 30 years we have experienced many sad situations. Most of them didn't have humorous elements to lighten the heaviness of loss. As I write this, I can't help but think of yesterday's funeral that Ash and Gwen held for a 46 year old neighbour here in Birmingham who drank herself to death. There were only five people at her funeral. What a privilege and a tragedy to be part of a lonely person's life and be there until the tragic end. It makes me very sad that these tragic situations continue to happen in our so-called 'modern world'.

Looking back, I now know that in those first three months in Thailand (and, to be honest, for most of our twelve years there) I made many clumsy mistakes trying to adapt to Thai cultural practices around death. For example, when I was working at the AIDs hospice I would sometimes bring Amy across to play with the patients. She was this cute blonde toddler and was really great for lifting everyone's mood. But I discovered the Thais themselves would never enter a hospice willingly. It was considered bad luck. Taking Amy caused a lot of gossip in Klong Toey, with everyone thinking I was a terrible mother. But sometimes even the mistakes worked out OK. Later on, one of our neighbours started to visit her brother in the hospice and when she told me it was because I wasn't afraid to take Amy there, I felt so relieved.

Even after an amazing three months in Klong Toey, we had no firm plans to move there. We stayed true to our commitment to spend five more years in Springvale, expanding the team there and setting up locally led churches for our neighbours who came to faith. But a year later, Ash was invited to attend a conference in the Philippines and in transit, stopped off in Bangkok to take gifts to Blah's family and the friends we had made there. As he arrived in Klong Toey, Ash knew instinctively it was home. Walking in (because taxis *still* wouldn't drive in) he felt God say: "This is where you should be."

When he arrived back in Springvale, he didn't know how to tell me. We were so settled back into our lives there. However, when he did, I burst into tears of joy! It had been my dream all along and now Ash had a clear vision for it too. But it took another two years to fulfil our commitments and fully handover to our Springvale team to continue the work without us.

It was a much harder process telling our local friends we were moving on. I had started to think we would be in Springvale for a long time with them – so felt deeply guilty about leaving. I dealt with this by insisting that we would still stay in touch, be back regularly and that nothing would change. That type of thinking is a coping mechanism for me, as I am terrible at emotions and goodbyes. The reality is that I give my heart and soul completely to what is in front of me. That means that over time I don't have the capacity to keep up the intensity of previous relationships, investing fully in the people in my present. I'm sure this is a personality fault. It has led people feeling hurt and left behind both in Australia and Bangkok. However, it also allows me to wholeheartedly invest in my current life with the community I am now rooted in. I really admire (and covet) faithfulness and steadiness in others. But unfortunately it's something I can't seem to master in myself. I do think God knows all our flaws though, and planned a path for me that played to my strengths. It does take certain types of people to start new things from scratch, and I guess my intensity in the present moment has been helpful in this. Although I'm not always great at showing it, I profoundly value and love people and relationships in my past.

I remember sharing the idea with our beloved 'Uncle Roy'. He was an ex-serviceman and junk collector, who, after having a vision from God telling him to feed hungry children, had been at one of Ash's talks. He became our office receptionist – even though he was quite deaf, but his great Cockney rhyming slang almost made up for the mixed up phone messages, and everyone loved this larger than life character. He was an important part of our family and much-loved by Amy and Christine as their favourite uncle Roy (helped by the fact he looked quite a lot like Santa!) At this time, he was living with us in Springvale. "I don't want you to go", he said. "I want you to stay here with us, but I can tell it's God's purpose for you and I shouldn't stand in the way." Roy in his graciousness released us to go to Bangkok and start a new team there. It felt a little self-indulgent; who wouldn't want to go and live in Bangkok and have an adventure? While I always desire to be guided by God and my faith community, I wonder, at times, if I may be guilty of using the God language to justify what I was already planning to do.

It took two years to be ready to leave. We needed to raise financial support, finish my paid employment as a crisis social worker and for Ash to secure an office space for the remaining team. As Ash was the main fundraiser for the organisation, it was important that we left the team with a secure budget, and a space they could call theirs rather than the little industrial office we were renting. There was a Mexican restaurant up for sale, in just the right place, and we were convinced it was the right place. However, the sale fell through. We felt devastated and let down. A few weeks later the real estate agent rang: "I've found what you need – it's a house in the community that has been used as a Buddhist Temple with large rooms, outdoor space and great lighting – perfect for your projects." The American Inner Change Team generously donated the deposit, and we secured a special loan from the Church denomination we were part of. Incredibly generous supporters had come forward, some who still faithfully support our work to this day.

People's generosity with both their time and finances continues to have the ability to floor me! The trust many supporters have placed in us is humbling to say the least. At each juncture in our 30 year journey, loyal givers have backed us and made our whole adventure possible. These people are often not the wealthy investors you might expect, and in most cases they give sacrificially out of a shared desire to see the world become a better, fairer place.

When we arrived in the UK, our son Aiden loved to tell people how we had to take money from a family in the slum and a Thai woman in a wheelchair. Which was true. In the weeks running up to our final departure from Thailand, there were so many farewell meals planned for us. Actually, it made leaving feel a whole lot worse. But I knew that people needed this time to process that we were leaving them; and some even needed to tell us how angry they were about it. One of these meals was hosted by our very good friend and cook extraordinaire, Poo. She was one of the first of my neighbours to work with me on setting up a social enterprise. When we were saying goodbye, Poo cooked a huge meal for the community. As we were leaving, one of Poo's sons, called Best, handed me a cloth bag with £2,000 cash inside. "This is for you to buy a car!" I pressed it back into his hand, "I can't take your family's money, Best!" I was so shocked by the size of the gift. "Yes you can, Anji! You always tell us the poor need to give! We have three cars now because you helped make our cooking business a success. You have to take this to help you in the UK." The truth was; we did need their generosity. We were going to the UK with little more than four bags of clothes. I accepted the money with sincere gratitude and did as I was told.

It was around the same time that a woman named Earth asked to meet me for lunch. Earth has quadriplegia, which makes life very difficult for her in Thailand. But we discovered that she was a brilliant translator. Her life was a struggle, but she began earning good wages as a translator and we employed her regularly to translate for the staff training days. She handed me an envelope and said: "This is for your family to use. Not for ministry!" Inside the envelope was 8000 Thai Baht, a month's wages for a day worker. It was humbling and embarrassing to say the least, but Earth insisted I take her gift. I always enjoy being the one doing the helping and giving and that's because it always feels nice to know you have helped someone. How dare I stop other people from having this same rewarding feeling? Aiden knew how embarrassed I was at being the person receiving help and still takes every opportunity to tell his version of the story to tease me.

We found a similar generosity among the poorest people when we landed in the UK. People like Yanis, a homeless 65-year-old Polish man. He had lived and worked in the UK for 14 years, mainly off the grid, paid cash in hand. But he had developed sciatica and other health problems so scraped by without any income at all for just over a year. He was made homeless so moved into a squat where he was treated as a slave. He had tried to apply for benefits but was told he was fit for work. Yet every time he tried to work, was laid up in agony afterwards. His mental health was deteriorating and he had lost hope. We began to help him reapply for benefits and secure housing. It took four advocates at Newbigin House 12 months to sort out his paperwork. Eventually it was decided that having worked so long in the UK he was entitled to pension credits, some of which was back paid. The first thing Yanis did when he was paid was to go out and buy Ash and I expensive fountain pens as a thank-you gift for our persistence. He lavished gifts on Gwen and Susie too. I wish I had taken a photo of the look on his face when we unwrapped his extravagant gifts in front of him – it was pure and perfect joy. Yanis continues to enjoy giving us gifts as if it is his greatest joy. So far we have received: a rocking horse, a suitcase, a bongo drum, a trolley and many decorative plates and books – all delivered to our door with great effort as he struggles to walk and can be seen dragging our latest gift up the road.

In every community we have lived in we have been blessed by people who have the least material possessions, but the biggest generous hearts. Actually, the generosity of the poor often shames the meagre attempts of those who have far more resources to share.

In all my decision making – from major life altering continental relocations – to internal dilemmas about the ethics of accepting extravagant donations; I try to trust that God has guided my decisions. Although I often feel like I'm stumbling in the dark.

Chapter 28 – I Believe in Miracles

Klong Toey, 2012

I felt the panic rise. You have GOT to be kidding me. I cannot believe I have managed to lose the whole bunch of keys to the community centre, truck and motorbikes. I'd been getting in strife with the centre manager quite a bit lately as we introduced new staff and projects that she didn't always agree with. But now this time I have really done it!

Over the years, I've observed a real danger in telling sensational stories about places like Klong Toey. I have sat in meetings before where Christians tell amazing tales about the miracles they have seen God do in faraway places. Sometimes afterwards, my cynical side causes me to chase up the source to check for accuracy. I am sad when my doubts are confirmed and there's no real evidence or credible source that these 'miracles' ever happened. I'm not doubting that God does extraordinary things (I call them 'Type A Miracles') but, far more often than we like to admit, our prayers do not seem to be answered. And terrible things happen despite our faithful and earnest pleas for divine intervention. We just don't get invited onto platforms to tell those stories.

The team in Klong Toey knew that I was suspicious of mysterious miracle myths. We had a little house church meeting in our home and a guy called Jim was speaking. To listen to Jim you would think he had a hotline to God. Apparently Jim prayed and then God did miracles. Like getting him cable TV to watch his beloved Liverpool football team in the Premier League. I wasn't convinced that was down to God. More likely the man selling stolen cable TV. Another time Jim and his partner called me panicking because they ran a small laundry business and he had hung up a customer's very expensive Duvet on a bamboo pole and the stain from the pole had left a mark right across the duvet. They had been trying bleach and other stain removers all day but nothing had worked. I looked up the brand on my computer and we were all shocked at how much it would cost to replace it. He prayed hard and about half an hour later they called me back ecstatic. After leaving the duvet to soak in water the stain had gone completely. Another miracle ... right?

Six months after I lost the Community Centre keys, I was still kicking myself. My absentmindedness incurred the wrath of my boss, thinly veiled behind an ever present Thai smile. Not to mention I inconvenienced many people while keys were being re-cut. So one night at our house church I rolled my eyes as Jim was sharing yet another random miracle that had supposedly happened to him that day. It sounded more like Santa Claus than God to me! So in order to start a conversation about this I said: "Isn't it unfair how God always seems to answer just Jim's prayers? Why couldn't he answer my prayer to find the community centre keys or something else useful like that?" Jim piped up that I should have more faith and suggested everyone to close their eyes and ask God for a miracle, stressing the importance of keeping their eyes closed as God won't answer your prayers if you don't. A bit baffled by this caveat, I shrugged and went along with it. We all sat in a circle and started to pray silently. I can't remember what my prayer was – I was probably preoccupied with another, more recent, drama. But when I opened my eyes, there in the middle of the circle was my lost bunch of keys! It turns out Jim and another staff member had found them earlier in the day wrapped up in the Christmas costumes and set the whole thing up. Everyone laughed and laughed; including me.

My friend Bun sitting next to me did not know the backstory to the keys and missed the fact it was all an elaborate joke. It was only her second time at our little church gathering and she grabbed my hand and whispered earnestly, "Anji, can you pray for me too. I haven't seen my daughter for ten years. Pray she comes back to me!" I didn't know what to say but I did what most cornered Christians do – I prayed a kind of half-way prayer, remembering to include the phrase "Lord if it's your will" just in case God did not answer her prayer as she wanted because I didn't want her to be disappointed.

Just days later, I was standing outside the community centre with my teammate Jodie. Along came an excited Bun, with an embarrassed young woman walking down the street towards me. It was her daughter. Home after ten years! Her prayer had been answered and Bun was elated. The temptation I always have is to 'be more Jim', to leave the story there. A nice, neat 'Type A miracle'. A feel-good testimony. And certainly Bun's prayer was answered that day. God showed up for Bun, just as her daughter did. But the story wasn't happily ever after. After a few days Bun's daughter noticed her mother taking HIV medication. She knew this meant Bun was HIV positive. Fearing she would be left to care for her mum, she took off in the night. To this day Bun has not seen her again.

It's important we tell the whole story. That's what I have committed to do in this book. Because if any of you set out to try and bring hope to the most hurting places, your story won't be full of Type A miracles either. But, even when you cannot see how God is present in the misery and chaos of the broken world, there's a different type of miracle that can happen if you let faith transform the pain inside you. It's the 'Type B Miracle'. This is where the situation does not change for the better; but you do. You lose some of your ego, some of your need to control, your urge for self-preservation and, hanging on to faith, you stay alongside those who are suffering, sharing their pain. It's a true miracle when you can do that.

Bun's story actually helped me overcome my doubts that God still does miracle A's. But it also left me knowing that regardless of the outcome, somehow we need to keep going and believing that one day there will be an end to all the pain and suffering in this world. We can stand still and let it roll over us like waves, or we can fight and hope that eventually the swell diminishes. The fortitude to survive whatever comes our way is surely the miracle God creates in us, and also through us, when we share our strength with others who have lost theirs.

Chapter 29 – The Missionary Position

Flight to Santorini, 2019

The dread builds up and I can feel my throat closing. I'm staring out the window, amazed by the vastness of God's creation but, kind of wishing I never got on this plane. Why did I ever suggest this stupid idea? Why didn't I just have a 50th birthday party? I'm excited about Greece and lovely sunshine and beaches, but feeling very awkward about the idea of writing my story.

Asides from my hyperactivity and a busy schedule, if I'm honest, the real reason I've delayed writing this book is the fear of being judged and of seeming 'cringey'. Recently I saw a meme that said: *"Courage is doing something even though you know it will hurt. Stupidity is the same and that's why life is hard."*

Perhaps you will be way less judgemental of me than I have always been of myself. I hope so. My wish is that by exposing some of my deepest thoughts and cherished stories, it will encourage others with much better stories than mine, to write them down. If the effort and pain of vulnerability in sharing my life experiences encourages even one person to take a risk and chose to live life alongside the poor in this world, then it is all completely worth it to me.

I know full well that I have had serious failings along the way and, after 30 years, I still make bad decisions and make poor word choices on a regular basis. But that's the whole point in this book! By laying it all out there I'm hoping others will feel encouraged that God can even use our worst mistakes.

While we are now enlightened enough to see the damage the 'white saviour' complex can cause, I wonder can there still be something noble in the concept of somehow using our privilege to help others? Poverty and injustice can be so overwhelming. It's often easier to criticise people trying, and doing it wrong, than it is to take a risk and try something yourself. How can this grotesque poverty and inequality continue to exist when you and I have way more than we actually need? Are Jesus' words for the poor just words? Or is it a physical demonstration of solidarity and provision that we are inextricably linked to?

There are times when I wonder if there even is a God. I worry that I have been misguided to choose to live and serve the way I have all these years. But in the end, even if God is not real, poverty and injustice is. I can not think of a more rewarding way to have spent my life than trying to do all I can, with what I have, to try and fix it. I'm pretty sure I couldn't have survived any of this work, and certainly not for 30 years, unless God gave me the strength. For that reason alone, I think that there is a God who loves us and grieves over this messed up world. Regardless, whether my faith proves to be right or wrong, I have no regrets either way.

God says:

"This is the kind of fast day I'm after:
to break the chains of injustice,
get rid of exploitation in the workplace,
free the oppressed,
cancel debts.

What I'm interested in seeing you do is:
sharing your food with the hungry,
inviting the homeless poor into your homes,
putting clothes on the shivering ill-clad,
being available to your own families.

Do this and the lights will turn on,
and your lives will turn around at once.

Your righteousness will pave your way.
The God of glory will secure your passage.

Then when you pray, God will answer.
You'll call out for help and I'll say,
'Here I am.'"

The Bible (Isaiah 58:6-9)